Publishing Informati

1st Published April 2020

Photographs taken by AJ Noon or A Venn unless otherwise credited.

Maps from OpenStreetMap: see www.openstreetmap.org/copyright

© **OpenStreetMap contributors**

CONTENTS:

Welcome

Welcome to Volume 1 of the Trafalgar Times, a collection of the first four issues, with added content to enhance and expand upon the information provided.

If you are new to The Trafalgar Times, then many thanks for taking the time to introduce yourself to us. We send free copies of the quarterly issues to schools, and to organisations with a naval/ Trafalgar/Nelson connection. For the first week of release each new quarterly issue can be found for free on Kindle. Any monies we take (such as you buying this) go to covering the costs of printing and to sending out a maritime/history related book parcel to a random school each quarter.

The aim of The Trafalgar Times is to introduce fans, and potential fans, of the Age of Sail to many different facets of this time in small, bite-sized chunks, providing links and ideas for the reader to then go and do further research should they wish.

There are many, many, serious and in-depth publications out there on these topics. We are trying to provide something that, although 'lighter', is as engaging and accurate as possible.

If you have suggestions for us then please do not hesitate to get in touch, traftimes@gmail.com, @traftimes for Twitter and Facebook.

Again, many thanks for taking time out of your life for us. Now, sit back, pour a tot of rum, and read on...

AJN & AV

The Trafalgar Times

Issue #1
Jul/Aug/Sep 2019

Gauging the Range

Hello, and welcome to the first issue of "The Trafalgar Times", a newsletter designed to capture and share interesting stories, facts, and reviews.

We intend to focus on HMS Victory, Vice-Admiral Nelson, the Battle of Trafalgar, and events of that age, but we will share articles on anything that will hopefully be of interest to those who dream of wooden walls.

The plan is to produce this newsletter every quarter, and we are hoping it will become a tool for sharing information amongst our fellow enthusiasts. One word of caution though: if you are expecting highly detailed, thoroughly technical articles, then there are plenty of places that already exist to sate your appetite (which we will tell you about). We aim to give you snippets and tasters, all accurate, but our mission is to dangle 'bait facts' in front of you, which you can then take further in your own explorations and research.

So, get your marker pen ready, and hopefully by the end of this newsletter you will have highlighted at least one article that has piqued your interest and you want to investigate further.

AJN and AV

A Beginning and an End

It does not seem right to start our first print-run with bad news, but unfortunately we must. We have just seen that the Nelson Museum, in Great Yarmouth, is going to close sometime around the end of October this year.

It has been open for the last seventeen years, and contains over two thousand items relating to Nelson and is based around a collection owned by Ben Burgess, who set-up a trust for the items, but declining visitor numbers and a lack of funding have contributed to its demise.

As well as letters and items of Nelson's, it has paintings relevant to his life, letters from his brother-in-law, and a huge collection of commemorative memorabilia associated with the man and his victories.

This has only just been announced, and at the time of printing we only know that the collection will go in storage until a solution is found. As it could be some time before the artefacts are displayed again, we strongly recommend finding the time to visit the museum before it closes.

It costs £4.25 for adults, £2.50 for children, but is not open on Saturdays.

We'll be organising a trip up there soon to do a review before it closes, but as the next issue comes out at the start of October, get your road-maps and your driving gloves out for a visit to Great Yarmouth.

There are a couple of other museums in Great Yarmouth with maritime connections (the Lydia Eve Steam Drifter trawler, Caister Lifeboat Station, and the Time and Tide museum), so you have extra options to see if you visit.

https://www.nelson-museum.co.uk/visiting.html

AJN

WHATEVER HAPPENED TO... JOHN RICHARDS LAPENOTIÈRE (1770-1834)?

Lapenotière, a Devon lad, is perhaps best known for his exploits as Captain of schooner HMS Pickle (10), and bringing the first news of Trafalgar to England. But what happened to him afterwards?

After much effort (and letter writing to William Marsden, first secretary of the Admiralty), he finally received a reward of £500 (roughly £30,000 today).

He was then given command of the brig HMS Orestes (16), and participated in the Battle of Copenhagen in 1807. He was promoted to Post Captain in 1811, but never received another commission and never sailed again in command of a ship.

He died in 1834 and is buried at Menheniot in Cornwall. Two of his three sons joined the Royal Navy, and he also had eight daughters (from two marriages, his first wife died in 1804).

AJN

"When I follow my own head, I am, in general, much more correct in my judgement than following the opinion of others." Nelson

PILLAR TALK

In the early hours of the 8th March, 1966, an explosion rocked Sackville Street, Dublin. When the dust had settled, a seventy-foot high granite protrusion now stood where there had once been a one-hundred-and-twenty feet pillar with a statue of Nelson on top.

Unlike Nelson's Column, the Pillar had an internal spiral staircase which led to a viewing platform below the statue (and yet was still cheaper to build than Nelson's Column in Trafalgar Square), and had stood since its completion in 1809 . The statue was sculpted from Portland stone by Thomas Kirk, and there were references to Nelson's battles etched into the base of the Pillar.

The edifice survived the Easter Uprising in 1916 intact, despite British artillery fire targeting the area, and after the Irish War of Independence (1919-1921) calls came for either its destruction or relocation, and by 1966 there were serious doubts about its in-situ future.

Its' bombing, responsibility for which was claimed by a former IRA member in 2000, scrapped any chance of it being moved, and on the 14th March the remains of the pillar were destroyed in a controlled explosion by the Irish Army.

The site remained empty for many years, until in 2003 the Spire of Dublin, designed by Ian Ritchie, opened. The sculpture is a three-hundred-and-ninety-foot stainless steel spire, looking much like a colossal pin.

When the army destroyed the remains of the Pillar, onlookers rushed to grab souvenirs, and luckily the head of Nelson eventually made it to the Gilbert Museum in Dublin.

I think the biggest loss for Dublin is the Pillar itself. Though it may not have had the greatest architecture (thanks to the builders keeping the costs down), having a viewing platform some one-hundred-and-sixty-eight steps up was a major tourist draw and, I feel, still would be.

AJN

(For some good images and detail see: https://www.olddublintown.com/nelson-pillar.html *)*

WALKING TRAFALGAR: PORTSMOUTH

Portsmouth City Council have a walk called 'The Nelson Trail' which takes you past key buildings and sites associated with Nelson prior to his leaving to re-join the fleet before Trafalgar.

There are fifteen points highlighted on the walk, but it is important to note that the walk is less than a mile in length, so is more akin to a trip to the shops. Starting from the Landport Gate, where Nelson would have entered Portsmouth, the path heads along the High Street and down to the Spur Redoubt, which is close to where Nelson's barge would have been waiting to return him to HMS Victory. You finish the tour by passing one of HMS Victory's anchors on the promenade.

If you are in Portsmouth, it is a must do, and maybe if you incorporate the Millennium Promenade Trail you can add some extra interest, and just enough distance, to justify a pint or an ice-cream at the end of it. The Millennium Trail starts by the main gates to Portsmouth Historic Dockyard and is marked by a chain etched into the pavement. This trail takes you down through the old Gunwharf (now a shopping centre but it retains some of the historic buildings you can view from the outside), and down to the Spur Redoubt (as found in the Nelson Trail). You will get a good view of the harbour movements, the old fortifications, and also the tower where the artist WL Wylie had his studio in Tower House along the way.

AJN

The Nelson Trail:

https://www.visitportsmouth.co.uk/downloads/dmsimgs/Nelson_Trail_leaflet_956402279.pdf

The Millennium Promenade Trail:

https://www.visitportsmouth.co.uk/things-to-do/millennium-promenade-p276841

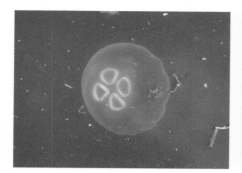

WILDLIFE: BASIN NO. 1

If you have visited HMS Victory in the warmer months in the last few years, you may have noticed the wildlife that thrives in the relatively contained environment behind the ship that is Basin No. 1.

My particular favourites are the two types of jellyfish: the Moon jellyfish (Aurelia aurita), and the Compass jellyfish (Chrysaora hysoscella). They can be seen in the sea as well, particular in the sheltered area between HMS Warrior and its' jetty, but Basin No.1 appears to be most acceptable to them.

Moon jellyfish can grow up to 40cm in diameter and are very common in the UK, and the four circles in the centre (upper left picture) are their reproductive organs. They have very short tentacles and the sting from them is mild (though not welcome).

Unlike the Moon jellyfish, the Compass jellyfish (upper right picture) visits the UK in the summer to feed, but be warned as these critters sting.

A couple of us swear we have also seen the flashing blue of a kingfisher heading towards the far wall of Basin No.1 (near where the PFC logo has been sprayed). We know they nest in a similar environment in Chichester, Emsworth and Poole harbours, so hopefully we will have some definitive sightings in the future.

AJN

A DIAMOND IN THE ROUGH

So, it is 1803, and you have a five-hundred-and-seventy-foot tall lump of basalt just outside one of the main routes into Martinique that is of no use except for foraging whilst blockading Fort Royal Bay and Saint Pierre Bay. Unless you can think of a better use for it.

Commander Sir Samuel Hood (1762-1814) did, and he had his men haul two 18 pound guns to the top, a 24 pounder into a cave near the middle, and a couple more 24 pounders at the base. Then they built fortifications, stashed supplies, and topped it up with a garrison of one-hundred-and-twenty men. The only thing needed was a name, so he commissioned it as the sloop HMS Diamond Rock, what is affectionately known as a 'stone frigate'.

Lieutenant James Maurice was placed in charge, and for seventeen months he happily used HMS Diamond to disrupt trade in and out of Fort-de-France until the end of May 1805, when one Admiral Villeneuve and his allied fleet happened to be in the area.

Villeneuve had orders to capture Diamond Rock, and after a two-week siege he finally landed troops on May 31st. The British troops, low on supplies and out of water, finally surrendered on June 3rd, with two killed and one wounded, though they took out three gunboats.

The prisoners were repatriated to Barbados, and Lt. Maurice had to go through the indignity of a court-martial for losing his 'ship'. The court-martial cleared the British of any wrong-doing, and Maurice went on to command an actual ship, rather than a rocky outcrop.

It is said the Royal Navy still salute Diamond Rock if they pass, but I have not managed to verify this yet.

AJN

EDUCATIONAL RESOURCE—KS2 ENGLISH AND HISTORY

The National Maritime Museum (Greenwich) has a teacher resource pack available online that covers the Battle of Trafalgar.

Coming in at nearly thirty pages, it covers KS2 History and English, and is primarily aimed at school groups attending the museum, but it has some interesting details and there is no reason why it could not be easily adapted for visiting HMS Victory, or even for giving some extra details and inspiration when you are taking your family to either of these attractions.

It covers the experience of an individual (John Franklin on the Bellerophon), the battle of Trafalgar, and a brief bit about women onboard ships at the time.

Anyone taking KS2 students to either Greenwich or Portsmouth should peruse this beforehand.

You can find the resource here:

https://www.rmg.co.uk/sites/default/files/Trafalgar_Tales_resource.pdf

AJN

CORRECTIONS

As this is the first issue, there are no corrections or retractions to tell you about (and long may this continue).

If you do spot something that is incorrect, or you feels needs clarifying, then please do not hesitate to get in touch with us.

traftimes@gmail.com

THE BROAD ARROW

From weapons and ammunition to food, stores and supplies, the broad arrow could be found on hundreds of items onboard a Royal Navy vessel throughout the age of sail. Also known as the 'crow's foot', usage of the mark can be traced back as early as the 14th century, being largely adopted by the 16th century to mark property owned by the government. It is said that the symbol was used in order to identify the origin of goods that were likely to be stolen. It is well known for featuring prominently on the uniforms of prisoners in Britain from the mid 19th century.

The broad arrow was also adopted by colonies across the British Empire, namely in America and later Australia. It was used both to denote exiting property of the crown, but also to earmark potential property seized by the British. This even included marking trees intended for use in shipbuilding as masts in the American colonies.

For those wishing to identify which of the minority of HMS Victory's guns are the real deal, the broad arrow is clearly visible on top in the centre of the barrel. The mark can also be found on some of the window frames around the buildings of the National Museum of the Royal Navy in Portsmouth.

AV

THE BATTLE OF TRAFALGAR: SAM WILLIS

56 PAGES £8.99

One of the latest entries into the Ladybird Expert series, Sam Willis' Battle of Trafalgar joins a line-up that includes the Spanish Armada, the Battle of the Atlantic, and the Battle of the Nile. It is worth noting that, for this series, Penguin appear to rely on the same experts, so if you find one in a style you don't like, then this is likely to be repeated.

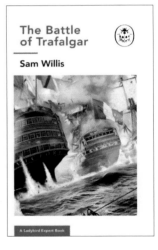

The narration starts with Napoleon crowning himself King of Italy, and finishes with the building of Nelson's Column. It does not follow a truly linear timeline, jumping around to different events in Nelson's career, Napoleon's conquests, and in the history of the Royal Navy, and because of the relatively dry telling of these events, it does not necessarily make a cohesive read at times.

The book lacks detail in places where it could really use it—shot types, women at sea, and the 'great chase', for example—but overall, it has some interesting sections. It does provide a good starting point if you are trying to get a younger reader interested in the battle and the characters involved, but as an adult (at whom these books are nominally aimed at), it falls far short.

The word selection at times is poor (the description of the final moments of Hardy and Nelson seems to be deliberately ambiguous), the swapping between Imperial and Metric measurements for no apparent reason, and the generalisation of numbers can all be frustrating for anyone who already has a basic interest in the battle.

It is well produced, and has some very good artwork that should help spur the younger imagination, but I feel it lacks a few pages of details. As a stocking filler to get someone started on the path of wooden walls, it is ideal, but it does not add anything if you possess even a basic library.

AJN

History Extra interviewed Sam Willis about this book:

https://player.fm/series/history-extra-podcast/the-battle-of-trafalgar

It is interesting (in this interview) how much the author appreciates the efforts of Collingwood over Nelson during the battle, but as the battle had been raging for some time before he received word of Nelson's death, how much influence did Collingwood have over the fighting?

DID YOU MISS? ADMIRAL (2015) 128 MINS

Available on both DVD and Amazon Prime—and originally entitled *Michiel de Ruyter*— *'Admiral'* brings to life the 17th Century Dutch Admiral, the key moments in his life, and the events leading to his death.

The sea battles are the highlight of the film, and though they may not explain his tactics clearly (which may be lost in translation, and is nothing which a bit of internet searching cannot resolve), they are engaging to watch. The scenes of his life and the politics that shadowed him throughout his career can be a bit tedious and not necessarily conveyed clearly enough to someone who is not a Dutch history master, but we do get appearances from both Charles Dance and Rutger Hauer to help bring some gravitas to the scenes.

Frank Lammers plays the Dutch hero, who is engaging enough to watch, and Roel Reiné, with a career rich in episodic tv, directs.

Though not a Napoleonic piece, anyone with an interest in wooden walls might enjoy this—just don't mention the Medway and the Royal Charles!

Be warned, as this is subtitled so it will need your full attention if your language skills are lacking.

AJN

Admiral — Just don't mention the Royal Charles!

LEGO TRAFALGAR SQUARE #21045 £79.99

Lego have a new release in their Architecture series, and this time it is Trafalgar Square (21045). The set has 1,197 pieces and retails at £79.99 (though it can be found cheaper with a bit of internet searching).

The set contains features including the front of the National Gallery, Nelson's Column, a representation of the fountain and the lions, and two London busses and a black cab. Be aware though, if you are not familiar with the Architecture series these are all microscale representations, with the London Bus being five studs high and three studs long.

It is a satisfying build, and it has some clever touches, such as the stairs in the square, and the trees. The rear of the Gallery has three removable panels so you can see some 'artworks' inside, but the set is let down by the lack of detail for the four panels at the base of Nelson's Column, and for the lions themselves (and Nelson has two arms, see the picture on the right). To build, it took just under two-and-a-half hours, but I do build a lot of Lego so you may take a more leisurely approach construction.

Overall, it is a clever set and looks good when displayed, but maybe wait for a price drop rather than pay the full eighty pounds.

NB: Nelson's Column also appears in the Lego London Skyline set (#21034, £44.99, 468 pieces). This set has far less detail (see the picture bottom right), but can be picked up for less. The skyline sets are quick builds, averaging an hour to do, and do not take up as much shelf space as the larger models such as Trafalgar Square.

AJN

PODCAST PEARLS

There are a number of podcasts available online covering Nelson, Trafalgar and the wider Napoleonic period.

For those who prefer listening to reading, various volumes of recordings of Nelson's letters to Lady Hamilton can be downloaded from iTunes. Be warned however, as we found that the voiceover at times does not make for the most enjoyable listening experience!

https://podcasts.apple.com/tn/podcast/letters-lord-nelson-to-lady-hamilton-volume-i-by-nelson/id417893744

BBC Radio Solent's H2O podcast featured HMS Victory in an episode originally published in 2015, in anticipation of the ships' 250th anniversary. It is 45 minutes well worth listening to, providing copious amounts of history and information on Nelson's flagship.

https://www.bbc.co.uk/programmes/p02pkf28

There is an episode from 2004 from the BBC Four 'Great Lives' series that focuses on Nelson. It features Terry Coleman, author of *Nelson: The Man and the Legend*, and covers Nelson's childhood up to his death at Trafalgar. Bear in mind that new scholarship has been unearthed and new debates surfaced since this was originally recorded fifteen years ago.

https://www.bbc.co.uk/programmes/b00768p

AV

THE TRAFALGAR TIMES

The Trafalgar Times is a publication put together to share information primarily focusing on the Royal Navy around the time of the Battle of Trafalgar. This scope, however, is not limited, and we aim to cover media and events that may appeal to anyone who has an interest in the age of sail.

If you have any suggestions, article submissions, or corrections then please email us:

traftimes@gmail.com

🅕 🐦 **@traftimes**

THREADING THE ROPES

You're on deck, there is a storm lashing the ship, and you and your shipmates are hard at work hauling in the bowline. A shout from above carries over the storm and the men in front of you reflexively drop to the deck.

You follow their lead, and you hear the whip-crack of a rope somewhere overhead as it gives way under the strain. The officer-of-the-watch shouts at you to grab the loose end that is dangling just above you, and you reach up and grab it, realising just how close it came to taking your head off. Peering at the rope, and despite the driving rain, you can clearly see the rogue's yarn running through the middle. It is a red thread and you curse under your breath at the journeyman roper from Plymouth dockyard who had made this piece, threatening your life with his poor work.

Okay, so the rogue's yarn was as much for detecting theft as it was for allowing defects to be tracked, but by 1780 all Navy cordage had a white thread laid through it so anyone caught with the rope could be identified as a thief. This was then refined to have a colour that signified the maker: Devonport dockyard used red, Chatham used a yellow thread, and Portsmouth used a blue thread. Is this related to the Portsmouth Football Club home colours you ask? Probably not as their first home shirts were pink and white!

There are records that show the Venetian Navy were adding coloured markers to their ropes as far back as the 14th Century. In the 20th Century the use of colours and patterns to identify cordage, continued and there are now European standards to harmonise this. For example: blue for Polyester and orange for Polyethylene, as well as manufacturer's patterns incorporating these colours.

The rogue's yarn is also known as the "thief mark."

AJN

> *"My dog is a good dog, delights in the ship and swims after me when I go in the boat." July 1790, Cuthbert Collingwood (1748-1810)*

'MONEY FOR OLD ROPE' AND 'CAPPABAR'

Two phrases that are linked, but one is problematic:

'Money for old rope' has long been said to have derived from the activity of breaking down old rope into oakum, which could then be used for caulking or sold when a sailor was on land. Picking apart ropes was also used as a punishment, and a task performed in Victorian workhouses, where overseers and owners would profit from selling the oakum made from old rope, thus giving us the saying...

Except: there is no written record of this phrase until the 1930's, yet one would expect to find this phrase somewhere in print in 'The Sailor's Word Book' of 1867 and onwards—but there is no sign of it anywhere.

So, for the moment, we have to use caution when relating this word back to the sailing navy. It is more than likely it was in oral use before being first written down, but for how many years?

'Cappabar' is the misappropriation of government property, and as most navy assets were marked with the broad arrow (see above for the identification of ropes), being caught selling on property would result in a severe punishment. 'Capabarre', an earlier form of the word, is mentioned in 1818, and is in 'The Sailor's Word' book. It also has a variant of 'capper-bar' and if anyone has some linguistic feedback as to the origins of these three variants then we would love to hear from you.

(Please note: 'cappabar' in any spelling format is not a valid Scrabble word should you try and play it!)

AJN

The Trafalgar Times
@traftimes

Issue #2
Oct/Nov/Dec 2019

Welcome

We are pleased to present, for your perusal, the second issue of the Trafalgar Times.

After receiving some great feedback and suggestions, which we are incorporating where possible, we have grown this issue slightly. It is still the aim of the *Trafalgar Times* to provide nuggets of information, rather than in-depth technical analysis, to help engage and inspire our readers to do their own reading and research.

We have been able to freely distribute over two hundred printed copies to schools and organisations in the UK, and we will continue to do so each quarter. To help improve on this distribution, and to engage more people with our passion, each new issue of The Trafalgar Times will be available in the Amazon Kindle store to download for free for the first week of each quarter. So please add a reminder in your calendars and let any other interested parties know.

Our Facebook, Twitter, and YouTube accounts are all up and running, and you can find us on these platforms using **@traftimes**.

Finally, we have also sent out our first little book bundle to a local school and with your help there will hopefully be more of these every quarter.

So thank you for your support so far and enjoy our second issue.

AJN and AV

A Time to Remember

Trafalgar Day: a day for remembrance and reflection, and the most important day in Victory's calendar. It is a day that starts like any other with the raising of 'Colours', as the White Ensign and Union flags are hauled up. This is shortly followed by the raising of the signal flags that spell out Nelson's famous *"England Expects ..."* message. Finally, a garland *'globe'* is suspended above the brass plaque on the Quarter Deck and everything is ready for the ceremony that follows.

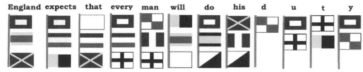

England expects that every man will do his d u t y

Attended by senior Royal Navy officers, the ceremony opens with Admiral Collingwood's General Order of 22nd October being read out by Victory's CO, which he then follows with a bidding giving thanks for the life of Lord Nelson. The Second Sea Lord then reads out Nelson's Prayer, and the Chaplain leads the company in a prayer of thanksgiving for the victory of Trafalgar.

This is followed by The Lord's Prayer, the Naval Prayer and finally the Naval hymn, 'Eternal Father'. After a short blessing by the Chaplain, the Second Sea Lord lays a wreath where Lord Nelson fell. A Royal Marine bugler then plays the Last Post and Reveille. The ceremony concludes on the Orlop when three wreaths are laid at the spot where Nelson died.

In the evening, a dinner is held in the Great Cabin where the guest of honour rounds off the meal by giving a short speech, followed by a toast to the *"Immortal Memory ..."*. In 2005, the 200th anniversary of Trafalgar, the toast was given by Queen Elizabeth – *"The immortal memory of Lord Nelson and those that fell with him"*.

SW

WHATEVER HAPPENED TO...

JEANETTE CAUNANT?

Unfortunately, we just don't know.

Jeanette was onboard the French *Achille* at Trafalgar, disguised as a male sailor to be with her husband. When the *Achille* went down - and after suffering burns from molten lead - she was rescued and taken to *HMS Pickle*.

She was fed and clothed before being transferred to *HMS Revenge* a day later, where she was given her own segregated area.

Luckily, her husband had also been rescued and taken to the same ship, and there they were re-united.

Each of the *Revenge's* officers gave her a silver dollar to help her, but when the Spanish prisoners were transferred at Gibraltar, she was accidentally (being French) released as well.

After that, we just don't know where she went—unless you know better...

AJN

"First gain the victory and then make the best use of it you can." Horatio Nelson, August 1st 1798

FOUND IN THE LIBRARY

When you tuck yourself into the library for a day of research, you always hope you are going to find exactly what you are looking for, written down in a legible script that clearly states all the facts you are after.

Unfortunately this never happens, it is always a case of piecing together multiple entries from multiple logs, cross-referencing, and sometimes a leap of faith to get you to the required result. But what I do love, especially on the days when evidence is thin, is when you stumble across something that has no relevance to your current research, but shows the humanity of the lives you are delving into.

Many a Captain, Lieutenant, and midshipman, made side notes, sketches and more in their logs, and these can be an absolute joy when you find them. For example, the sketch below is from the log of a midshipman on a British frigate attempting to intercept a ship near Porto Santo in the early 1800's.

Finds like these, whether they are sketches, details on punishments, gunpowder recipes, or just a question mark against an order that was issued—they all make a day of research worthwhile.

AJN

P.S. Remember if you are reading a ships' log, a day starts at midday, not at one minute past midnight!

WALKING TRAFALGAR: GREENWICH

More of a stroll than a walk, this trail takes you around fifteen spots in the Greenwich Naval College area that have links to Nelson, ending up in the main Nelson gallery within the National Maritime Museum itself.

The trail includes the Painted Hall (when it is open), Hardy's Mausoleum, and Chantrey's bust of Nelson (one of which is at Windsor Castle, but is not currently visible). If you are not planning to do the museum then the walk itself is too short on its' own, so you may want to stroll along the Thames to add some distance to earn your pint. There is a downloadable version of the trail on the following link:

http://nelson.greenwich.co.uk/things-to-see/

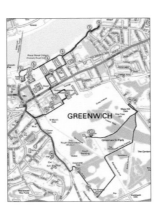

Personally, I prefer to do this walk in reverse, starting within the museum and walking through the grounds towards the Thames—though I really couldn't guess as to my motivation for this! Okay, I lie, you have to visit The Trafalgar Tavern if you are in Greenwich!

If you want a longer walk, with more sailing and less Nelson, then take a look at the 'Discovering Britain: Exploring the Ends of the Earth' tour (see left), which is similar to the above walk but adds in the *Cutty Sark*, Sir Walter Raleigh, William IV, General Wolfe, and more.

http://tiny.cc/yllwcz

AJN

SPANISH SHIP-BUILDING

The battle of Trafalgar undoubtedly had a profound effect on Spain and its Navy, eventually leading to the severing of ties between the country and Napoleonic France. However, whereas its former ally continued to hold a large naval force, Spanish shipbuilding faltered to an unprecedented low point.

The Eighteenth century Spanish navy was a force of considerable strength, boasting some of the largest ships of the line in the world, including the 140 gun *Santísma Trinidad* (right). Spanish vessels tended to be larger than those of the Royal Navy, with a good core structure, however during the wars in the latter half of the century Spain lost 79 ships of the line. This left the Spanish navy with only one 74 gun ship, four frigates and around thirty smaller vessels by 1844. Whereas around one-hundred and fifty ships were launched in Ferrol in the latter half of the eighteenth century, in the following half century this number had fallen to less than a dozen.

Of the seventy-nine ships mentioned above that were lost, twenty-two were lost in action, ten by accident, eight were repossessed by the French and thirty-nine were condemned due to their poor condition. France took control of major Spanish ports such as Cadiz, taking with it any warships in the harbour. Spain also suffered from their trade to the Baltic and North seas, which they relied on for vital imported shipbuilding materials, being cut off by Britain during its post-Trafalgar economic warfare with Napoleon.

Following the end of the Napoleonic wars, the Spanish shipbuilding industry was slow in growth, and also late to adopting steam power. No new ship was built during the reign of Ferdinand VII, which ended in 1833, and the only additions to the fleet were purchases from Russia. Although these foreign imports were cheaper and appeared to be of better quality than the domestic product, the Russian squadron was scrapped not long after purchase due to their poor construction. Spain would go on to eventually build their first post-Trafalgar ships of the line in the early 1850s.

AV

PIERCING THE VICTORY

HMS Neptune (1874-1903) was an ironclad turret ship originally designed and built for the Brazilian navy as *Independencia*. As tensions grew with Russia, she was purchased by the Royal Navy in 1878 in case of war breaking out. *Neptune*, however, never saw action, and was sold for scrap in 1903. Shortly afterwards, on 23rd October, she finally made a name for herself.

Whilst being towed out of Portsmouth harbour (which someone decided was a good idea to attempt during a storm) the tow cables broke. *Neptune* drifted free, bouncing off the side of the brig *Sunflower*, before puncturing the port side of *Victory* and finally coming to rest against the *Hero*. Luckily, the crew onboard *Victory* were alert and the *Victory* was eventually taken into dry dock for repairs.

As you can see from the photo on the right, the damage, though penetrative, could have been far worse.

HMS Neptune (above) made it to the scrapyard in 1904, and with three ships called *Neptune* at Trafalgar, it feels as if the Roman god of the sea was having one more attempt at getting hold of *Victory*. The damage done was one of the factors that influenced *Victory* being put into drydock permanently, though this did not occur until 1922.

AJN

TIMELINE TREMOR 001

December 16th, 1793, and the French are in the process of recapturing Toulon, which they have besieged since the 9th of September. Napoleon Bonaparte himself, a mere commander at this time, leads a counter-attack on a battery held by the British, and during this encounter the timeline of history must have quivered as it worked out which way it was going to flow.

A sergeant from the 18th Royal Irish Regiment bayonetted Napoleon in the leg, leaving him with a wound severe enough for amputation to be considered—the future of the man who wanted to be Emperor lay in the balance: if his leg was amputated, his stellar military career would likely never have happened, and the Napoleonic Wars may well have been the Ney Wars or the Blücher wars.

Fortunately for Napoleon (though not for Europe), his leg was saved and, after fighting off a severe infection in the wound, Napoleon continued on the path that would send Europe into another round of turmoil. The wound did trouble him at future times, and there is reference to the scarring in his autopsy reports, but it did not end his career as it initially threatened to.

We do not know the name of the Irishman on whose bayonet history balanced, but we wonder if he lived to know he was the man who almost stopped Napoleon.

AJN

BOOK REVIEW: BATH AND NELSON

112 PAGES £10.00 THE NELSON SOCIETY

If you had asked me about Lord Nelson's connections to Bath before I had read this book, I could have told you there were some, but not necessarily enough for a whole book on the subject.

Then I read this, and I can say that there are, just, enough for a publication. Covering names, places, and dates, sometimes in a tumble of words that would have benefitted from tighter editing, this book has a wealth of information tucked away in its pages.

It follows (roughly) the historical timeline, but it does have some branches and missteps that distract from the read. Having said that, it really helps bring detail to not only Nelson in Bath, but the whole social scene that navy officers and their wives had to contend with.

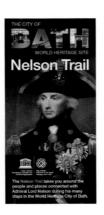

The book would have benefitted from a few more period drawings and images of Bath, rather than the more modern photos of the buildings as they are now, as this would really help to set the Georgian scene.

There are four chapters (of the twelve) towards the end book which list contemporaries and Trafalgar sailors with links to Bath, details on a phial said to contain liquid from the barrel that transported Nelson's body back to England, and wraps up with a walking tour and relevant map.

If you have an interest in Bath, or the social scene that Fanny would have had to contend with, then this book is for you.

AJN

DID YOU MISS?

It's back! Twenty-five years after first being launched, Stephen Biesty's magnificent Man-of-War cross-sections book has been updated and relaunched. With cutaways including food, work, battles, sleeping, and navigation, this is a must for any youngster who wishes to know more (or whom you wish to inspire). It has details on sayings, superstitions, and more included in its diagrams.

Priced at £14.99, and despite only having thirty pages, this book has a huge amount of information crammed inside its covers. Buy it now, either to remember your youth or for future generations.

AJN

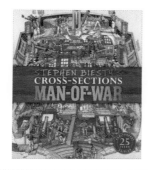

FOUND (AGAIN)

You may have read that the wreck of *HMS Endeavour* (1764) is thought to have been found off Rhode Island, USA. Though this wreck was first discovered in 1993, it is only now they are starting to believe she is the *Endeavour* (later known as the *Lord Sandwich*), and not another wreck that is only a few miles away, which they now think is *La Liberté,* formerly *HMS Resolution* (1771).

If this is the case, this is two of Cook's round-the-world ships in the same relative area.

A good article on the wrecks here:

http://tiny.cc/45fvcz

And here for the ship and expedition:

http://tiny.cc/sdmbdz

http://tiny.cc/7gmbdz

AJN

"...of all the figures on the Castlegate, none were more picturesque than the dulse-wives."
Charles Dickens, 1856

NATURE: SHORELINE STORES

You find yourself walking along the beach, approaching a port to sign up on a ship, and you take a few minutes to search the shoreline, looking for some essentials to take with you. As the year is 1784, and you can't rely on the ship you sail on to have stocked up with limes, sauerkraut, or onions, you know you should take with you whatever you can forage. Some men eat the rats they catch, and they rarely seem to get scurvy, but you will most likely never get a chance to get into the hold to catch any. The thought that rats make their own vitamin C is alien to you.

You spot what looks likes a mass of dried white bubbles, about the size of your fist, and you quickly pick it up, brush the sand off, and drop it into your sack. Within five minutes you have a few more stashed away; 'sea-wash balls' are always useful, as not only do they act like a sponge when you wash with them, they also produce a lather to help get you clean. They are actually the discarded egg cases of the common whelk, a familiar sight along our beaches.

Next, on the rocks near where the waves are breaking, you can see dulse growing, which you pick and wash off in the water. Once dried, you can chew it like tobacco, and if you knew about Vitamin C you would realise that it has a high content to help prevent scurvy, but you do know that it is good for when you have a hangover.

On a clump of dunes, just inland, you spot some pine trees. You can make a very good restorative tea from pine needles, you just need to make sure you don't pick up any needles from the yew tree, which you know to be deadly. As before, you are unaware of Vitamin C and its power to prevent scurvy.

Of course, the plant you really want to find is a variety of scurvy grass (right), and you soon spot some poking up through the dunes. Oddly though, you will only start taking this when scurvy takes hold, not as a preventative, and there is talk that even the Romans used it.

You finally reach the town and head to the port, hoping that your foraging will help to keep you healthy over the coming months at sea.

AJN

NB: Please be carefully if you do forage, and be very sure of what you are collecting and how to prepare it.

THE WINDSOR BALL

The musket ball that did for Nelson is on display at Windsor Castle, though it is in a temporary location at the moment.

It can currently be found in the Lantern Lobby—just after St. George's Hall—and is on the bottom shelf of the left-hand cabinet as you enter.

Unfortunately, the Chantrey bust of Nelson is, at time of going to print, inaccessible. However, the Nelson bust in the arches outside the National Maritime Museum in Greenwich is a copy of this one.

Tickets for Windsor are £13 for a child and £22.50 for an adult, though we would not recommend going during the summer holidays as it gets *very* busy.

AJN

15

CHRISTMAS GIFT SUGGESTIONS

We know you may be reading this on the first of October, and we apologise, but as we are quarterly our suggestions for Christmas have to be in this issue. We could not find any Admiral Nelson socks—and we did look—so here are some other suggestions to go on your wish lists:

NMRN Minis Rum and Gin

The National Museum of the Royal Navy have an online shop from which they sell Pusser's Gunpowder Proof Rum mini's (70cl, 54.5%, £6.99), and as we all know sailors need their rum!

They also sell a HMS Victory Gin (70cl, 57%, £5.00). Both are perfect stocking fillers—adults only of course.

https://shop.nmrn.org.uk

Admiral Nelson Rubber Duck, £8.99, Amazon/Ebay

For someone who needs an Admiral for their bath-time navy, then the Nelson Rubber Duck is a perfect gift. Or if you want to recreate their affair, there is also an Emma Hamilton one available.

Airfix HMS Victory, 1:180 Scale, RRP £32.95

If you want to give a younger modeller a good challenge, or bring back someone's youth, then Airfix is always a reliable one to turn to. This kit comes in at 38cm long, so makes a decent model, though the builder may find the rigging a tad tricky if they don't have a steady hand or the best eyesight. With this kit, remember it comes with no building tools, glue, or paints, so if you are buying this for someone who hasn't built one in a while it would be worth buying it from a model shop so you can get the required accessories at the same time.

Airfix also do a smaller starter kit that comes with glue and paints, but it only has 19 parts and is 10cm long—though this may make it a good stocking filler.

eBay: Battle of Trafalgar Stamps and Coins

If you want to put a little more time and effort into the present selection, then sit yourself in front of eBay for a while and have a look at some of the Battle of Trafalgar stamps and coins from around the world that you can find there.

For the coins, we particularly like the Cook Islands series commemorating Trafalgar, and you can get these in a base metal version or in silver (check carefully which you are paying for). They would be good for individuals to gift each one, resulting in a full set for the recipient.

The Gibraltar 2005 First Day Covers (with stamp and coin insert) also make a nice set, and would look very good displayed.

Royal Mail Royal Navy Ships Stamps Collection

The Royal Mail have just released a stamp series on the Royal Navy, and have some nice framed options. There are eight ships, going from the *Sovereign of the Seas* (1637) to the new *HMS Queen Elizabeth* carrier. There are a range of presentation options, including the single framed ship and stamp sets at £39.99, and a presentation pack at £11.20.

https://shop.royalmail.com/

Hopefully we have given you a few ideas to help in your gift giving.

AJN and AV

TRAFALGAR SHIPS 001: HMS ACHILLE

HMS Achille, a two-decker Pompée class of 74 guns (16 x 9lb, 30 x 18lb, 28 x 32 lb), was launched in 1798 in Gravesend. In her first seven years, prior to Trafalgar, she spent much of her time in the channel fleet, and not too much of note happened—though in 1799 she was in a collision with *HMS Caesar*, damaging her own bowsprit.

On March 31st, 1805, Captain Richard King took command of the *Achille* and he eventually used his influence to be transferred to Nelson's fleet, with the ship joining Nelson the day the combined fleet left Cadiz.

At Trafalgar, with a crew of 640, the *Achille* was seventh in Collingwood's line, engaging first the *Montanes*, then the *Argonauta*, then the French *Achille*, and finally the *Berwick*. The *Berwick* surrendered to the Achille after losing approximately half of her 500+ crew to death or injury, whilst the *Achille* only lost 13 men with 59 injured.

In July 1812 the *Achille* was involved in an action off Venice, where her boats assisted in capturing twelve trabaccolos (two-masted cargo coasters up to around 200 tons and few guns).

She had a major refit in 1817-1822 to round her stern off, improving her rear protection, but she was placed in ordinary afterwards, and was finally scrapped in 1865.

There is a detailed history of the ship, and plans, at this link: http://tiny.cc/ubredz

AJN

FITBIT WOES

You've spent the morning wandering around HMS Victory, covering every deck multiple times. Out of curiosity you glance at your Fitbit and see it has only logged you climbing two sets of stairs, yet surely you must have done at least twenty?

There is a simple reason: for Fitbit to track a *'floor'* you must ascend ten feet, whereas Victory's deckheads are less than ten feet apart.

So if you want to spend the day wandering around a ship **and** to get an accurate stair-count, you will need to find a slightly more modern ship to explore.

AJN

1750: When Westminster Bridge opened, and an Englishman first used an umbrella (allegedly)

1750: ENGLAND VS FRANCE BOARDGAME REVIEW

Battle Hardened Games, RRP £23.99, 2 Players Only

The first thing to note about this game is that it has a limited sailing navy aspect to it. The second thing to note is how good everything looks—all the artwork is taken from paintings and sketches of the period, giving the game a very atmospheric feel.

It is a card-based conquest game, with each player taking on the role of either England or France as they attempt to expand their interests in the four zones across the world (the Caribbean, North America, Africa, and India). You recruit troops and generals, positioning them where they can both defend your existing holdings and conquer new ones, with locations giving you resources to convert into gold to spend on new armies.

There are only five turns each in this game, which may seem too few, but we played three games for the review and each time it played differently, with a game averaging fifty minutes to complete. The rules also come with alternate versions, such as setting up the initial colonies with historical accuracy, rather than randomly.

As you play the game you quickly get a feel for it, and there are side missions and diplomatic options to fulfil for bonus points.

This game is enjoyable, beautiful looking, and though appearing simple to play can leave you cursing as you watch your armies be defeated by a reinforced castle your opponent sprung on you.

The biggest drawback is that it is only for two players, but we both recommend keeping an eye out for this.

AJN and AV

RECIPE: NELSON CAKE

A bread pudding dedicated to Nelson, which saw an upturn in popularity during World War II as a way to use up stale bread.

Ingredients

225g Stale Bread (in pieces, no crusts)

300 ml Milk

1 tbsp Brandy (of course, and no barrel required!)

50g Melted Butter

50g Soft Brown Sugar

2tsp Mixed Spice

175g Mixed Dried Fruit

1 Egg (Beaten)

Lemon and Orange Rind

Nutmeg (grated for the top)

Method

Turn the oven on to 180C (or 160C for a fan oven).

Soak the bread pieces in the milk for around half an hour, add the egg, butter, spices and sugar and mix well with a fork.

Stir in the fruit and grated rind, put into a buttered ovenproof dish, and sprinkle the grated nutmeg over the top.

Place in the oven and leave to bake for between 75 to 90 minutes. Once cooked, sprinkle some caster sugar over the top and serve.

AJN

THE TRAFALGAR TIMES

The Trafalgar Times is a publication put together to share information primarily focusing on navies and events around the time of the Battle of Trafalgar. This scope, however, is not limited, and we aim to cover media and events that may appeal to anyone who has an interest in the age of sail.

If you have any suggestions, article submissions, or corrections, then please email us:

traftimes@gmail.com

 @traftimes

---

HOW MUCH IN A TOT?

Rum... did it get its name from the Dutch *Roemer* glasses, the Elizabethan *'rum booze'*, the latin word for sugar *'saccharum'*, or *rumbullion* from Devon? Well, we don't know for sure, though you can find arguments for and against each possible source. The same applies to the earliest brewing of rum (as a sugarcane based spirit). The earliest written evidence comes from Barbados in 1650, so it must have been a few years before this that it began production.

The navy officially adopted it in 1655, when Vice-Admiral William Penn captured the then Spanish colony of Jamaica. The initiall ration of rum was half a pint, though this was raised to a full pint in 1731 with the argument being it would encourage the men to put more effort into their work!

At this time, rum was stored on ships in *'overproof'* strength. Because the rum would often be stored alongside gunpowder on smaller ships, if it leaked it could not be allowed to affect the volatility of the powder, so by being *'overproof'* (57% ABV/114 proof) if it leaked in storage, you are not going to affect your fighting ability. When the rum was purchased it would be tested by mixing it with a small amount of gunpowder and seeing if it would still ignite. If the rum was weak the gunpowder would not flash, so this also helped to ensure the purser was not being ripped off.

Grog comes in thanks to Admiral Vernon in 1740, when he has the rum watered down at a ratio of four to one, allowing the ration to be split over two issuings a day, rather than just one. There are some sketchy reports that he was adding lime juice and spices to the rum at this point but this, if true, would have been done by the men, not him. The Royal Navy does not officially add sugar and lemon or lime juice to rum to counteract scurvy until 1795.

In 1824, the size of the rum ration was taken down to half a pint, then a quarter of a pint in 1850, and then finally down to an eighth of a pint (71ml/2.5 ounces). That is just over a double UK shot (70ml) at 54.6% ABV (95.5 proof).

One of the darkest days in the Royal Navy was July 31st, 1970, when the last rum rations were issued, on the day now known as *'Black Tot Day'* (the New Zealand Navy managed to hang onto their rum ration until 1990 though!).

So whether you take your rum neat, or in a cocktail such as a daiquiri (which is pretty much how the sailors were drinking it in the late seventeenth century, though in a somewhat less refined form), or you try and smuggle it onto your ship inside a coconut, rum will always be associated with the Royal Navy.

AJN

> *"Our country will, I believe, sooner forgive an officer for attacking an enemy than for letting it alone."* Horatio Nelson, May 3rd 1794

A COAT OF GROG

Admiral Edward Vernon (1684-1757) is the man who gave birth to, and gave his name to, grog. Sailors used to call him *'Old Grog'* as he wore a grogram coat, which is a material made from silk and mohair, and has a corded appearance. It often has a coating of gum to improve its waterproofing, thus increasing its weight, and Vernon preferred it to the finer coats that might be expected of a senior officer.

In 1740, when he ordered that water be added to rum to help combat drunkenness amongst sailors, the new mixture was called grog after him.

But grog is not the only thing the Admiral had named after him: Porto Bello Road in London, which now has a famous clothes market on it, was originally called Green's Lane. In 1739 Vernon, with a fleet of just six ships, captured the Spanish-held town of Puerto Bello (now Portobelo) in Panama. This led to great rejoicing back in England, and Porto Bello farm was built and named in 1740 in honour of the victory.

Not only that, but the victory helped inspire *'Rule, Brittania'* in 1740 as well, though luckily it is not called Rule Vernon, or similar.

In 1741, things did not go his way in an attack against Cartagena, Colombia, and he was forced to withdraw, but that was not enough to tarnish his name.

Ignoring the multiple pubs still out there, Vernon had several ships and the torpedo training school in Portsmouth named after him—of which *HMS Warrior* (1860) was part until the site moved ashore, where it replaced the gunwharf which had been there since 1706. The whole site is now a shopping centre, with the Spinnaker Tower presiding over everything, though some of the Georgian buildings have been preserved inside the complex.

Some people have speculated that if Nelson had not come along, then Vernon would be the most well known British Admiral of the age, but what about Jervis, Anson, or Rodney?

And if you are wondering what happened to the signage from HMS Vernon... It's on the wall of the *Rum and Crab Shack* in St. Ives, Cornwall.

AJN

The Trafalgar Times

@traftimes

Issue #3.01
Jan/Feb/Mar '20

Welcome

Welcome to Issue #3 of The Trafalgar Times, and a happy 2020 to you all.

If you've been down to the dockyard in Portsmouth (England) in the last month or so, you will have seen a huge amount of activity with the settling in of the two new aircraft carriers HMS Queen Elizabeth and HMS Prince of Wales. Now, we cannot really count these as 'sailing navy', but the very first *HMS Prince of Wales (1765)* was a third rate and the second *HMS Prince of Wales (1794)* was a second rate.

The second *HMS Prince of Wales* was present at the battle of Cape Finisterre (1805), which was an important precursor to the Battle of Trafalgar, so we have an article on this ship inside.

We are continuing to ensure each new issue is free on Kindle for the first week of each quarter, and we are continuing to raise funds for the printed copies we send to schools and organisations, and for the small book parcel we send out to a random local school each month.

We do this in our own time, so if you do buy an issue, thank you. Now, get your daily rum ration ready, sit back, and enjoy.

AJN and AV

An Officer From Mansfield Park

In Mansfield Park (1814), Jane Austen's third book, there is a character called William Price who is serving as an officer in the Royal Navy, and it is believed she based this character on her own brother, Sir Francis William Austen (1774-1865).

Francis joined the Royal Navy in 1786 at the ripe old age of 12, and his first ship was *HMS Perseverance (35)* on duty out in the East Indies. He made Lieutenant in 1792, and was appointed to *HMS Andromeda (32)* in 1795.

In 1799 he took his first full command, the sloop *HMS Peterel (24),* and was involved in several large operations over the coming years. In 1805, in command of *HMS Canopus (80)*—captured from the French at the Battle of the Nile—he took part in the great chase as Nelson hunted Villeneuve and the combined fleet.

On October 2nd, 1805, Nelson sent several ships, including *HMS Canopus* to Gibraltar to re-supply, so Austen missed Trafalgar. He did get a chance to show his mettle at the Battle of San Domingo (now in the Dominican Republic) in February 1806, when seven British ships-of-the-line took on five French, and it was another decisive victory, with two of the French ships destroyed and three captured for no loss.

During his career he served in the Mediterranean, the East Indies, the West Indies, the Channel blockades, and he North Sea. In 1812 he captured the privateer *Swordfish* when in command of *HMS Elephant (74)*. He was also involved in actions against slave-traders in the 1840s. He was appointed Knight Commander of the Order of Bath (1837), and then Knight Grand Cross of the Order of Bath (1860). He had a good reputation amongst his crews, seeing to their welfare as much as possible, and was finally appointed to Admiral of the Fleet in 1863.

Though he outlived his sister, Jane, his letters and visits home must have provided ample inspiration for the character of William Price and her descriptions of his naval service.

He died at home in Widley, Hampshire, in 1865, leaving behind ten children. He was buried at the St. Peter and St. Paul Churchyard in Wymering, Portsmouth, though the grave is rather non-descript for one who reached the highest rank.

AJN

WHATEVER HAPPENED TO ADMIRAL VILLENUEVE?

Pierre-Charles de Villeneuve (1763-1806) was a commander who used up all his lick surviving Trafalgar, but he could not escape Napoleon.

During the French Revolution he quickly dropped the 'de' from his name but between 1793 and 1795 he struggled for a commission because of his nobility, but despite so many blue bloods fleeing or being executed, he survived.

At the Battle of the Nile in 1798 he failed to engage the British fleet with his ship, was captured a couple of days later, and then released.

At the Battle of Trafalgar, he was the only senior officer onboard the *Bucentaure* not to be injured or killed. Again he was captured, but this time brought to England, where he lived on parole in Bishop's Waltham, Hampshire, even attending Nelson's funeral.

Upon release he headed back to France, but Napoleon refused to see him or grant him a command position. Then, in April of 1806 at an inn in Rennes, Villeneuve's body was found. He had been stabbed seven times and was buried in an unmarked grave.

The coroner saw fit to rule it as suicide, but the consensus is that Napoleon ordered his 'removal' for his failure to defeat the Royal Navy.

AJN

"I wish to have no connection with any ship that does not sail fast; for I intend to go in harm's way." John Paul Jones

HMS PRINCE OF WALES (1794)

The second ship to carry the name, *HMS Prince of Wales* was a second rate ship of the line. Part of the *Boyne* class, she was built in Portsmouth and was launched and commissioned in 1794. As a second rate vessel, she held 98 guns and had a maximum complement of 750 men. With a hull length of 182ft and a maximum beam of 50ft 4in, she was five times shorter and just under five times thinner than her modern day namesake.

HMS Prince of Wales came close to seeing its first taste of action in the 1795 battle of Groix, though the ship was not engaged in this particular conflict. However, she would truly experience battle ten years later in Sir Robert Calder's action off Cape Finisterre on the 22nd July 1805. The ship served as Calder's flagship in the battle which, although classed as indecisive, played a large part in the lead up to the battle of Trafalgar. The British fleet engaged with Admiral Villeneuve's Franco-Spanish fleet, which had just sailed back across the Atlantic, having failed to achieve their aims in the Caribbean. In a largely confused and disjointed encounter, the British managed to capture two enemy ships and damage several others. *HMS Prince of Wales* suffered moderate damage to her masts and 3 men lay dead with a further 20 wounded.

As a result of this battle, Villeneuve's fleet eventually made its way to Cadiz where it remained blockaded until Trafalgar. Calder was summoned back to England for a court martial, and as a result, missed the famous battle. Nelson allowed Calder to return home in his flagship, and the *Prince of Wales* left the Mediterranean in early October 1805.

The ship spent a brief period as the flagship of Vice Admiral Lord James Saumarez in the channel in 1807, before fulfilling the same role under Admiral James Gambier for the expedition to Copenhagen (still 1807).

After a period in ordinary of three years from 1808, the *Prince of Wales* was briefly re-commissioned in 1811, before being laid up in the same year. She remained in reserve until 1814 and was ultimately broken up in 1822.

Her sister ship, *HMS Boyne*, caught fire and sank at Spithead off Portsmouth on the 1st May 1795. The site of the wreck is now marked by the Boyne Buoy in the Solent.

AV

WALKING TRAFALGAR: THE TRAFALGAR WOODS

In 2005, the 200th anniversary since the battle of Trafalgar, 33 new woods were planted around the United Kingdom, with each named after aa British ship-of-the-line from the battle and the six support ships.

The trees planted reflect the wood used at the time, such as silver birch which was used for the brushes, alder for charcoal (a gunpowder component), ash and oak. Most of the woods are relatively small, but the largest, the Victory Wood in Kent, covers 350 acres.

In Northern Ireland there are the Belleisle, Dreadnought and Euryalus woods.

TRAFALGAR WOOD SITES

1.	Defence	Moray
2.	Swiftsure	Perth & Kinross
3.	Belleisle	Fermanagh
4.	Dreadnought	N. Down
5.	Defiance	Dumfries & Galloway
6.	Royal Sovereign	Northumberland
7.	Ajax	Durham
8.	Revenge	N. Yorkshire
9.	Polyphemus	Lancashire
10.	Spartiate	Carmarthenshire
11.	Colossus	Herefordshire
12.	Mars	Warwickshire
13.	Achilles	Derbyshire
14.	Leviathan	Leicestershire
15.	Tonnant	Norfolk
16.	**Neptune**	**Oxfordshire**
17.	Prince	Suffolk
18.	Bellerophon	Essex
19.	Victory	Kent
20.	Orion	Hampshire
21.	Thunderer	Berkshire
22.	Temeraire	Hampshire
23.	Agamemnon	Hampshire
24.	Africa	Dorset
25.	Conqueror	Devon
26.	Britannia	Devon
27.	Minotaur	Cornwall

For some reason a full list of the sites and their location is proving difficult to obtain, but one tool you can use to try and track them down comes from the woodland trust: https://www.woodlandtrust.org.uk/search/ allows you to search by name, so just enter the name of the ship.

We'd love to see your pictures of the woods, so please tag us on FB or Twitter with @TrafTimes.

AJN

FAMILY FORTUNES

It is the 31st of May, 1762, and the Spanish frigate *Hermione* is nearing home after sailing from Callao, Peru. She is loaded with gold, silver, tin, and even cacao, and it is believed she did not know that England and Spain had been at war for five months.

Two British frigates, *HMS Active* (28) and *Favourite* (18), spotted her and closed in. After only a few broadsides being fired Captain Zabaleta in the *Hermione* struck his colours. You can imagine the surprise of the two British Captains, Herbert Sawyer and Philemon Pownoll (also under Pownell and Pownall), when they saw the contents of the hold. *Hermione* was taken back to Gibraltar and assessed for prize money, with **each** captain receiving £64,872, and the standard sailors receiving £480 each, making her the richest prize ever captured by the Royal Navy. For the seamen below deck, that money was approximately 30 years salary, paid in one go, whereas the Captain's payout comes in at over 13 million pounds in todays' terms (using the BoE inflation calculator). But the question is, what did the two Captains do with their money? Were they sensible? Was it invested? Or did they fritter it away?

After the Seven Years War ended (1763), Captain Sawyer (c1730-1798), of *HMS Active* did not go to sea immediately, enjoying his rich rewards for fourteen years. Due to a prior agreement, he actually split his prize money with Captain Charles Pierrepoint Medows (1737-1816). Sawyer finally went back to sea in 1777, dipping in and out of service until 1790, though his health deteriorated. He reached the rank of Admiral in 1795 (though not in command of a ship) and died in Bath in 1798. His friend, Medows (sometimes listed as Meadows) eventually became the 1st Earl of Manvers, with Thoresby Hall, Ollerton, Nottinghamshire their ancestral home, though this title died out in 1955. No doubt the money he received helped his political career as he only did seven more years of naval service.

https://morethannelson.com/officer/herbert-sawyer-1/

Captain Philemon Pownoll (c1734-1780), of the sloop *Favourite*, bought an estate in Devon, having Sharpham House designed and built for him by Sir Robert Taylor (1714-1788) and gardens designed by Capability Brown (c1715-1783). Pownoll went back to sea in 1774 and was active against American shipping, capturing ships in 1777 and 1778 in *HMS Apollo* (32).

In 1779, whilst engaging the French frigate *Oiseau* (26) off of Brittany, Pownoll was shot, with the musket ball lodging in his chest, where it remained until his death the following year. On 15th of June 1780, whilst engaging the French *Stanislas* (26), Pownoll was hit and killed by a round shot, with command falling to Lieutenant Edward Pellew who captured the *Stanislas*.

Sharpham House still survives and is used as a retreat and a wedding venue, whilst the estate produces the most excellent cheese.

https://historicengland.org.uk/listing/the-list/list-entry/1000701

https://sharpham.com/

So both men had more than enough money to never have to go to sea again, and both took a few years off to establish families, though it seems Pownoll achieved more with his, whilst Sawyer (with half the amount) seems to have frittered it away on a large family.

And the wives of the two newly minted Captains? They were sisters, the daughters of a Portuguese merchant!

AJN

NAILING YOUR COLOURS TO THE MAST

Upon entering battle, ships would often hoist the oversized battle ensigns aloft to allow for easier identification in the confusion of battle. If a ship lowered these ensigns (sometimes draping them over the stern of the ship) during battle, it was used to show that they were surrendering and would allow a boarding party onboard.

Ships would fly battle ensigns off of several masts to ensure that one being shot away would not then be mistaken for surrendering. At 20 foot by 40 foot these flags are huge, and one from *HMS Victory* was used to cover Nelson's coffin during the state funeral.

If a Captain was determined to not surrender his ship, despite the amount of damage taken, or he wanted to ensure that his colours could not be shot away, then the battle ensigns would be nailed to the mast, ensuring that as long as the mast was not shot away then the battle ensign would still show.

At the Battle of Camperdown (1797), Jack Crawford climbed to the top of the mainmast of *HMS Venerable* and nailed the colours to them to ensure they could be seen.

The saying we now use, "nailing your colours to the mast" to show you are sure about a course of action or a decision comes from the use of battle ensigns and not wanting to surrender or back down.

TIMELINE TREMOR 002

During the night of June 22nd, 1798, sailors onboard the French invasion fleet heading towards Egypt heard the sound of bells and signalling guns far out in the darkness. Panic must have set-in amongst some of those aboard the ships.

Though they had thirteen ships-of-the-line, they were escorting Napoleon himself along with around 280 transport ships, packed with 38,000 troops, horses, and supplies. Even the warships had been packed with extra supplies, which would have made fighting difficult.

The bells they heard came from Nelson's fleet, with the two fleets coming within thirty miles of each other during that night. If Nelson's fleet of 13 (Nelson was onboard his flagship *HMS Vanguard*) had sighted and engaged the French then could Napoleon have been defeated?

When the Battle of the Nile finally happened on August 1st, it was a decisive victory for the British, but the French were caught at anchor and felt relatively safe where they were.

If they had engaged the British at sea, then undoubtedly there would have been British losses, but with the French ships so heavily loaded their capacity to fight would have been reduced, and historians generally agree that it still would have been a British victory, with Napoleon captured or killed, and his army killed or captured.

So if it had been the British crews hearing the night bells, the Napoleonic Wars may never have happened.

AJN

BOOK REVIEW: THE ROYAL NAVY IN THE NAPLEONIC AGE—SENIOR SERVICE—1800-1815

PEN AND SWORD PUBLISHERS   MARK JESSOP   180 PAGES £19,99

Though only having nine chapters, we were really impressed with the eye for detail and the ability to dig out details that bring the events of the time to life.

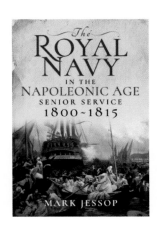

Each of the chapters starts with an imagined conversation or snippet from a battle to set the scene. Some of these work better than others, but each are pretty well imagined attempts to lead the reader into the action. The remaining bulk of each chapter then goes through the events, personalities, and concerns—of both Navy personnel and the general populace—of the time.

The chapters cover events such as the Battle of Copenhagen, Trafalgar, the slave trade, and shipwrecks, but always with a view from the side rather than head-on. Jessop is not afraid to highlight the issues the Royal Navy was facing at the time, such as embezzlement, theft, and examples of nepotism, and provides plenty of source material to reinforce this. It is always nice to read a book that does not go heavy-handed on patriotism and a veneer of whitewash.

This book is well researched and sourced, having 24 pages of index and 13 pages of references. There are also sixteen pages of illustrations and maps, some of which we were not too familiar with.

Overall, we feel this is a great addition to our library and we now have the urge to delve into the back catalogue to get a copy of Jessop's previous book covering 1793-1800.

AJN

DID YOU MISS? THE LOST FLEET

Back in 1999, the Discovery Channel created a documentary about the search for the L'Orient and from the Battle of the Nile. The documentary is an interesting mix of underwater archaeology and the history of the events leading up to, and including , the Battle of the Nile.

Unfortunately the documentary itself does not seem to have been released, but we have found a reasonable version on YouTube: https://www.youtube.com/watch?v=x2Lm7UmsKm8 .

The book that accompanies it however is stunning, with a serious collection of imagery

relating to the expedition of both Napoleon, and the Discovery diving team. It covers the build-up, the Battle of the Nile itself, Nelson, and details on the L'Orient as they such for it, as well as their end results.

Though the book has been in print for a while, you can find many excellent quality issues of it for sale on places such as eBay and Amazon. We paid £4 for ours and it is as good as new.

AJN

EDUCATIONAL RESOURCES #2

Two amputating knives, one metacarpal saw (and spare blade), six scalpels, two tenaculums (a type of forceps), a saw for the head: all these and more can be found in the naval surgeon's chest of 1812.

There is a complete list of instruments required, as well as some of the basic techniques used at the time, listed in an article by the Journal of Royal Society of Medicine.

http://tiny.cc/b921hz

The British Medical Journal (BMJ) have a similar article that supplements the above:

http://tiny.cc/ii31hz

AJN

"Pernicious weed! whose scent the fair annoys, Unfriendly to society's chief joys" William Cowper (1782)

TOBACCO TIMES

Take your allowance of tobacco, soak it in rum (to help keep it moist), wrap it in cloth, roll it tightly, then wrap it in twine to compress it. This gives you your 'prick' of tobacco, which was also known as a 'plug' or a 'perique'. Depending on the size of the ship, the only two places you could smoke were by the galley and on the fo'c'sle, and these were at set times. If you were a smoker a clay pipe would be your preferred instrument of delivery, and with these restrictions in place it was more common for sailors to chew the tobacco, with an experienced/careful chewer getting two days of use from a 'wad'.

You would receive your monthly ration in dried leaves, so firstly you would remove the stalks (which could be ground into snuff), and then prepare the leaves as above to moisten it prior to use.

You can see a prick of tobacco here: https://www.youtube.com/watch?v=cbk6w0Rl95A

In England we are commonly taught that Sir Walter Raleigh introduced tobacco to England in 1586, but Spanish and Portuguese sailors were using it before this date and we know that sailors worked wherever they could, so it is inconceivable that English sailors were unaware of it before this date. Before 1806 sailors purchased tobacco from the purser (with the money deducted from their wages at the end of the voyage when they were paid, and from 1806 they were given a ration of 2 pounds (weight, including stalks) of tobacco per month—if you did not smoke it was a valuable exchange commodity below decks. As always, wanting to be different and more socially accepted, officers preferred snuff and cigars.

But as well as smoking and chewing, tobacco also had other uses. From 'The Napoleonic Prison of Norman Cross', in reference to the prison hulks: *"If a ship in the Royal Navy had an outbreak of fever on board, it was the policy to fumigate the vessel... The fumigation was performed by smoking the ship with tobacco, often wetted with vinegar and containing sulphur..."*.

In 1818 The Naval Chronicle said: *"During the foggy season... the air is impregnated with un-wholesome vapours... fumigation should be frequently... the most simple we will suppose to be vinegar, sulphur, gunpowder, and perhaps tobacco.'*.

So, at the time, you could chew it, smoke it, set fire to it in a confined area, and trade it, whereas now we highly recommend you give it a wide berth.

AJN

FROZEN MONKEYS

It's freezing outside, and your grandad turns to you and says (much to the disapproval of your mother) "It's cold enough to freeze the balls off a brass monkey".

This is one of the more common phrases quoted to us, but we are confident it does not have a naval origin.

Allegedly, the tray on which shot was sometimes stored was made of brass and called a monkey. Shot was made from iron, so as temperatures changed the brass contracted at a different rate to the iron, thus forcing the shot (the balls) off of the monkey.

Well, we know shot was stored in shot garlands (wooden planks with hollowed receptacles) on the decks after being brought up from the shot lockers in the hold, and we don't see any literary references until the 1870's, and these talk about "freezing the tail off...".

As much as we would love that this great saying comes from naval traditions, it is very likely that its source is elsewhere.

Luckily we have hundreds of other sayings we know did come from the Navy!

AJN

WESTMINSTER ABBEY

Westminster Abbey has many naval memorials in it, and we wanted to highlight some of the ones you may miss or not be aware of, as well as the more obvious ones (NB: If you want to see the Nelson effigy and memorabilia you need an extra ticket for the Queen's Diamond Jubilee Galleries £5).

Admiral Sir Charles Wager 1666-1743): Captured the Spanish treasure fleet at Cartagena in 1708.

Edward Vernon (1684-1757): As mentioned in Issue #2, also known as Old Grog, captured Porto Bello in 1739.

Admiral Sir George Pocock (1706-1792): Fought during the Seven Years War, mainly in the Indian Ocean, captured Havana in 1762.

Vice-Admiral Sir Henry Blackwood (1770-1832): Captain of the Euryalus at Trafalgar, assistant to William IV after retiring from the Royal Navy.

Sir Peter Parker (1785-1815): In command of the brig Weazel that first saw the combined fleet preparing to sail from Cadiz in 1805. Involved in the re-capture of Île de France (Mauritius), died at the Battle of Caulk's Field, Maryland.

David Beatty (1871-1936): Although Commander-in-Chief of the Grand Fleet in WWI, he started his sailing career onboard the sailing ship HMS Britannia (previously the HMS Prince of Wales).

The Abbey has a great online search tool to help you identify and locate the hundreds of memorials:

https://www.westminster-abbey.org/about-the-abbey/history/famous-people-organisations

AJN

BURIED HOW MANY TIMES?

We were fortunate to find ourselves in Seville a couple of months ago, and of course we had to pay our respects to Cristoforo Columbo (1451—1506), whom you probably know better as Christopher Columbus. Inside Seville Cathedral is a hugely ornate tomb (technically a catafalque, a raised bier) containing his remains. But over the years not only have his remains been moved, but there was also some doubt as to which remains were actually his.

Columbus died in 1506 in Valladolid in Spain at the age of 54, with conditions such as gout, arthritis, and a lifetime of stress on his health from his travels being blamed as the cause. Initially, he was buried in Valladolid, but three years later he was moved to Sevilla to the family tomb.

When his son died, there was a clause in his will stating that Columbus's remains be moved, so in 1542 they were shipped across the seas to Santo Domingo, Hispaniola, which Columbus visited in 1493. Hispaniola (the Greater Antilles) finally ended back under Spanish control and in 1795 the bones were moved to Havana, Cuba. Finally, in 1898, they were taken back to Seville.

But that's not quite where the story ends. A lead box was discovered in Santa Domingo, with his name on, and for over 100 years there was a dispute as to who had the actual remains. DNA testing showed that the remains in Seville are more than likely to be those of Columbus, but the contents of the box in Santo Domingo have never been tested, so he may actually be in both.

AJN

TRAFALGAR SHIPS 002: HMS AFRICA

When you look at the belfry on *HMS Victory*, you will notice a small oddity. The casting date for her current bell is 1795. The original bell (and belfry) was shot through during the Battle of Trafalgar, and the current bell (currently on a permanent loan) came from *HMS Africa* (1781, 64 guns).

If you look closely at the order of battle for Trafalgar, tucked away at the very top you will see *HMS Africa*, all on her own and heading back to the line led by *HMS Victory*. During the night she had lost position and missed the overnight signals, so found herself isolated. To re-join her comrades she will have to sail past a third of the combined fleet, and Nelson, seeing the danger, sends signal 307 ordering her to pull back. Captain Henry Digby (later an Admiral of the Blue) decides he wants to be part of the action, so instead sails down past the enemy in the traditional line of battle formation—though with no support—firing broadsides as he passes each of the enemy ships.

Finally the *Africa* finds herself alongside the *Santissima Trinidad (134)* and, thinking she has struck her colours, Digby sends a boarding party onboard. Almost unbelievably, the Spanish admiral informs them he has not struck, escorts them off his ship, and the fight continues. Africa then engages the *Intrépide* which she takes with the help of *HMS Orion (74)*. By the end of the battle the two-decker had engaged four of the largest enemy ships and had taken quite a beating: remarkably she 'only' had 18 killed and 44 wounded from her crew of 498.

Sluggishness seemed to be a part of her general sailing characteristics as she not only missed the battles in India in 1782, but in 1812 she was part of the failed chase to catch the *USS Constitution (54)*.

She was heavily damaged during the Gunboat War in 1808 when 25 Danish gunboats attacked the convoy *Africa* was escorting. On this occasion she was saved by nightfall, and managed to return to Sweden for repairs.

She was finally scrapped in 1814 in Portsmouth, England. When he died in 1842, Digby was an Admiral of the Blue, had received the Order of Bath, and was Commander-in-Chief of The Nore.

Though *HMS Africa* wasn't the fastest, the largest, or the best-handling ship at Trafalgar, she certainly showed her courage for sailing down the line and holding her own with no support.

AJN

> "We have met the enemy and they are ours..." Oliver Hazard Perry

BY THE NUMBERS: GETTING YOUR PAINT OUT

Trawling through eBay, we came across various Painting By Numbers kits with a maritime theme, so in our Friday night wisdom we decided we would give one a try, and chose the one you can see on the right.

These things are cheap (less than £10) and come from China, so took a while to arrive, but once it did the quality of the canvas was better than anticipated, and it also contained 20 acrylic paints and three paint brushes. What did surprise us was how small some of the numbered areas actually were, no more than a splodge of a paintbrush in some places.

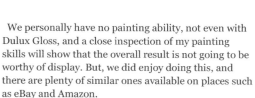

Undeterred by the age of our eyes (and using a portable backlit magnifying glass), we stretched the canvas onto a frame (not supplied) and set to work, with a podcast on the Napoleonic Wars running in the background.

Five hours later, we had done paints 1 through to 9 on approximately half of the canvas (see below), and despite the squinting it was surprisingly relaxing.

We personally have no painting ability, not even with Dulux Gloss, and a close inspection of my painting skills will show that the overall result is not going to be worthy of display. But, we did enjoy doing this, and there are plenty of similar ones available on places such as eBay and Amazon.

They do make quite a good stocking filler or small gift, though the addition of a frame stretcher and extra black paint is a must, and are a most relaxing pass time, even if we cannot get the paint inside the lines!

AJN

A SURGEON IN DISGRACE—ALMOST

William Beatty, *HMS Victory's* surgeon at the battle of Trafalgar, is arguably one of the most well known figures from the battle. He tended to Lord Nelson's wounds when he was brought down to the cockpit, and later wrote *The Authentic Narrative of the Death of Lord Nelson*, which provided a comprehensive account of all that happened on that fateful day. However, things could have panned out very differently for Beatty, who faced a court martial early into his career.

Beatty originally joined the Royal Navy as a surgeon's mate in 1791, earning promotion to surgeon in February 1795. He was posted to the 28-gun frigate *HMS Pomona* in March 1795 under the command of Captain Lord Augustus Fitzroy, a young aristocrat who had quickly (and questionably) risen through the ranks.

On the 19th July 1795, during a muster of the crew, Beatty and Fitzroy had a disagreement surrounding the health of two seamen. One of the men had been suffering from a bad leg and Beatty had recommended that he not walk on it. Fitzroy claimed to have seen the man out of his bunk and walking , and therefore disagreed with Beatty's assessment. The altercation escalated when Fitzroy accused Beatty of sending a disproportionate amount of men off of the ship to hospital and questioned his overall ability to conduct his duties. Beatty, furious at the accusations, exaggeratedly bowed to Fitzroy. The Captain took great offence at this and ordered Beatty be arrested and confined to his cabin awaiting court martial.

The court martial was carried out aboard *HMS Malabar*, with a panel of 12 captains assembled, including William Bligh of *Bounty* infamy. Fitzroy acted as prosecutor and called forward eight witnesses, including the first and second lieutenants. All witnesses agreed that they did not see anything wrong with Beatty's actions, and the panel exonerated him of all charges.

Beatty next took up the role of surgeon aboard the frigate *HMS Amethyst* in September 1795, and would go on to achieve fame at Trafalgar and eventual promotion to Physician of the Fleet. Fitzroy faced a court martial himself in May 1799, accused of disobedience and misconduct after failing to bring home a convoy he was charged with escorting. Ironically, he was declared guilty and was subsequently removed from command.

AV

"Don't give up the ship!" (Whilst mortally wounded in the fight against *HMS Shannon*) Captain James Lawrence of the *USS Chesapeake*

BLUE IS THE COLOUR...

Nelson: Rear-Admiral of the Blue. Vice-Admiral of the White? What is that?
Under the reign of Elizabeth I the British navy had grown large enough to be split into squadrons, with each squadron having its own colour. Unsurprisingly, the colours chosen were red (the centre squadron in a full formation), blue (the rear squadron), and white (the Van), in that order of seniority.

This order changed in the mid 17th Century to Red, White, and then Blue (the lowest), and career progression was a set path: you would be promoted to Rear-Admiral of the Blue, then White, then Red. Then to Vice-Admiral of Blue, then White, then Red, followed by Admiral of the Blue, Admiral of the White, and finally Admiral of the Fleet (there was no Admiral of the Red at this point).

After Trafalgar in 1805 the rank of Admiral of the Red was introduced, but the principle remained the same: Rear-Admiral Blue then White then Red, Vice Admiral Blue then White then Red, Admiral Blue then White then Red, with the newly created Admiral of the Red eventually being promoted to the Admiral of the Fleet.

So, had Nelson, as Vice-Admiral of the White, survived Trafalgar, he was still four promotions away from reaching Admiral of the Fleet. Some of the men who reached this top position include Sir George Rooke (1650-1709), The Lord Anson (1697-1762), Sir Francis Austen (1774-1865, see front page), and Sir Henry Keppel (1809-1904). In more recent times King Edward VII (as Prince of Wales 1841-1910), Sir John Fisher (1841-1920), and The Viscount Jellicoe (1859-1935) have fulfilled the top role.

In 1864 the structure was changed completely, doing away with the Squadron colours, and the position of Admiral of the Fleet has purely been an honourary position since 1995.

Oh, and if you wanted promotion you would have to wait for an Admiral to die or be removed in disgrace, the position was for life!

AJN

A STICKY SITUATION

At the outbreak of the American War of Independence (1812), England was importing over 100,00 barrels of pitch and tar, with the biggest individual customer being the Royal Navy.

Pine tar, made from the roots and stumps of pine trees, is incredibly important to sailing navies, and became a valuable commodity in the 17th and 19th centuries. It is used as a preservative, on both wood and ropes, and as a waterproof sealant.

And, of course, it led to two legends. Firstly, the nickname for British sailors of 'Jack Tar', which comes from either the excess tar on their hands they picked up from handling ropes, and/or from using tar to waterproof their own clothes.

Secondly, it lead to the Royal Navy saluting differently from the other UK armed forces, with two key differences. As their hands were dirty, instead of saluting showing the palm, the hand is turned 90 degrees so as to hide any dirt. Also, onboard ship space is limited, so the Navy salute goes straight up and down, rather than coming up from the side:

http://tiny.cc/8241hz

If you want to know how to create pine tar, then you can find the process here: http://tiny.cc/ll41hz

There is an incredibly in-depth article, 'The Royal Navy's quest for pitch and tar during the reign of Queen Anne', which can be found online here: http://tiny.cc/hh41hz

AJN

THE TRAFALGAR TIMES

The Trafalgar Times is a publication put together to share information primarily focusing on navies and events around the time of the Battle of Trafalgar. This scope, however, is not limited, and we aim to cover media and events that may appeal to anyone who has an interest in the age of sail.

If you have any suggestions, article submissions, or corrections, then please email us:
traftimes@gmail.com

 @traftimes

The Trafalgar Times

@traftimes

Issue #4
Apr/May/Jun '20

Welcome

Well, we've actually re-written this introduction multiple times over the last eight weeks, but the pace of events in the world at the time of final editing (late March) makes it difficult to find something fitting to open with.

We have decided to leave our museum and attraction reviews in, even though most cannot be visited at the time of publication, in the hope they will inspire you to add them to your wish-list for when some normality returns to the world. We also apologise for the bad jokes included in this issue, but it is released on April 1st.

We know many educators, conservators, riggers, and craftsmen who are currently being forced away from their beloved ships and artefacts all over the world, and we hope that soon they will be able to return to work for when museums and ships can be visited freely once more.

Many sites have been adding virtual tours to their web-offerings, and we have linked to a few, but there are many more coming online all the time, so have a look around the internet and share with us, @traftimes, any great ones you find. The same goes for any useful educational resources you stumble upon (or have).

Stay safe everyone, and hold fast!

AJN and AV

BUCKLER'S HARD: BIRTHPLACE OF A FAVOURITE

Buckler's Hard Maritime Museum, in the New Forest, Hampshire, UK, is a little gem tucked away on the Beaulieu River. The village was originally built in the 18th Century, and the shipyard there built its first navy ship in 1744, HMS Surprize (24 guns). After the success of its initial contract, over forty navy ships were constructed there, including three of our favourites (no surprise why): *HMS Euraylus* (1803, 36 guns), *HMS Swiftsure* (1804, 74 guns), and Nelson's favourite, *HMS Agamemnon* (1781, 64 guns).

Shipbuilding ended there in the 19th Century, though during the Second World War it was used for building MTB's and as one of the many bases for Operation Overlord. Now the buildings have been restored and there is a Maritime Museum, workshops, living history displays on a regular basis, and river cruises (seasonal).

If you get there on a fair-weather day, you are in for a treat as it is a picture-perfect place, and the museum covers the history of the village and the ships they built with some detail. There is a fantastic model of *HMS Agamemnon*, and some Nelson artefacts as well.

If you are planning a visit then check out their events page first as you may want to visit during one of the re-enactment days. Tickets are cheaper online, and a yearly pass is also available. There is a pub and a café onsite, but if you have good weather taking a picnic is a good option. If you are travelling a distance to visit, you can find a hotel on-site and campsites nearby. Tickets are £7.50 for the site and museum, and the river cruise (when running) is £5.50.

This is a very pleasant and informative place to spend a day, and we visited when the HMS Pickle replica was present and Portsmouth Model Boat Display Team were re-enacting various events (see left).

https://www.bucklershard.co.uk/attractions/

AJN

WHATEVER HAPPENED TO... THOMAS SLADE?

The man who designed eight of the British ships (and two controlled by the French) at the Battle of Trafalgar, Thomas Slade spent his life working in the shipyards of Plymouth, Woolwich, Chatham, and Deptford.

His designs helped to standardise ship production, most notably the 64-gun third rates. He was Surveyor of the Navy from 1755 (until his death), and was knighted in 1768.

He died in Bath in 1771, and is buried in Ipswich.

Though HMS Victory is probably his most well known design, nearly a quarter of the British ships at Trafalgar were 'his': *Africa*, *Agamemnon*, *Bellerophon*, *Defence*, *Defiance*, *Prince* and *Thunderer*, and the previously captured ships *Berwick* and *Swiftsure* fighting on the French side.

AJN

*When Lord Nelson died he was 5'6" tall. His statue in Trafalgar Square is 17'4" feet tall...
That's Horatio of 3:1*

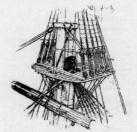

TIMELINE TREMOR #003: CHASING TAILS

July 16th, 1812, and the *USS Constitution* is en-route to New York to join up with Commodore John Rodgers' Squadron. The ship had been collecting fresh stores and crew in Annapolis when war with Britain broke out. It is early afternoon when lookouts first spot an unidentifiable ship to the northeast. Captain Isaac Hull gives the order to sail towards the unknown ship, thinking it to be part of an American squadron. However, four other ships are spotted in the vicinity of this unknown vessel and it soon becomes clear that these are British ships, namely *Aeolus, Africa, Belvidera, Guerriere* and *Shannon*.

Outnumbered, *Constitution* turns away from the enemy squadron and a chase ensues. Over the next couple of days, the American frigate and the British ships struggle with a lack of suitable wind. Isaac orders the crew to dump drinking water supplies to lighten the ship, and boats are dispatched by both sides to tow their ships along. Acting on suggestion from Lieutenant Charles Morris, Isaac also orders kedging to begin, with the ship being pulled along by pure manpower on the capstan. Both sides exchange shots, all missing their mark.

Then, on the 19th after a fifty hour chase, Isaac gives the command for the sails to be shortened to prepare for an incoming squall. Spotting this, the British ships react and do the same. In a stroke of genius, the *Constitution* then unfurls her sails, speeding away from her pursuers at 11 knots and taking full advantage of the conditions. Having been caught out, the British squadron gives up the chase the following morning.

But what if the British force had caught up to the *Constitution*, or if Isaac wasn't the shrewd tactician he proved to be? Would the *Constitution* now be moored in Portsmouth Harbour alongside HMS Victory as a museum ship, instead of in Boston? Or would she have been broken up and used for other purposes like *USS Chesapeake*? Perhaps *HMS Guerriere* and *HMS Java* would have survived the war instead of suffering their fates at the hands of the *Constitution* in *the coming months*? Maybe the loss of the ship would have been a demoralising defeat for the Americans that shattered their war effort?

If Isaac and the crew of the *Constitution* had not acted in such a manner, perhaps we'd now have one less surviving ship from the age of sail, or one with a completely different story and in different hands. Although it is unlikely that this one event would have changed the course of the war like the other timeline tremors in previous issues, it's interesting to envision what could have been the fate of the *Constitution,* had she fallen into British hands.

AV

WALKING TRAFALGAR: THE TRAFALGAR WAY

OFFICIAL STORYMAP (FOLDED) £19.99

The Trafalgar Way, the company who have mapped and researched the route that John Richards Lapenotière (1770-1834) took from Falmouth to London with the first despatch from the Battle of Trafalgar, have launched updated versions of their storymap, including a folded version (like an OS map, £19.99), a large wallchart version (£30), and a poster version (£15).

We bought a copy of the map version, and are very impressed with the amount of detail crammed into it. Not only does it contain an overview of the route, it has panels on the people and ships involved, and the most likely routes through town centres. It also lists the costs incurred for the journey, a timeline, and more.

We absolutely love the map version of this, and if you have an interest, or live in one of the places Lapenotière travelled through, then this, in one format or another, is an absolute must for your collection.

There is so much information on the map we are more than happy with our purchase; so much so we are thinking of getting our cycling legs out again this summer for a little challenge!

https://www.thetrafalgarway.org/storymap-product

AJN

LOSING HIS MARBLES

"Victory, at Sea, 2nd September, 1804.

Sir, Lord Elgin having requested through Sir Alexander Ball that I would allow a Ship to call at Cerigo, to bring from thence some marble antiquities...Nelson and Bronte."

Yes, *that* Lord Elgin and *those* marbles. We are not going to pass comment on the Elgin marbles themselves, or about their current location in the British Museum, London, but they do have a link to Nelson:

Thomas Bruce, the Earl of Elgin, set sail from Portsmouth in September 1799, heading for Constantinople where he was to be the ambassador to Ottoman Sultan Selim III. On the way to his new posting, Elgin met Nelson and the Hamiltons in Naples, where he described Emma as *"a whapper!"*.

On 6th July, 1801, Elgin received a firman, or authorisation, to survey and take casts of anything in the Acropolis. There was a line in this decree which Elgin translated as being able to take what he wanted as well, to be transported to England. Elgin's interpretation of this line (and liberal application of money) is one of the key points in the argument for the return of the Elgin Marbles now.

By 1802, around two hundred crates of marble and stone were taken to Piraeus and Elgin had been hoping that Nelson, with one or more of his large warships, would be at Piraeus to move and protect the shipments, but the British fleet had left before the crates arrived. The first 16 or 17 crates were therefore loaded onto the *Mentor (brig),* which then sank in a storm a few days after setting sail. *HMS Braakel* was employed to recover the treasures, and when the wreck was examined in 2011 it was found that all the crates had been removed during those recovery operations.

When the Napoleonic Wars broke out, Elgin was detained in France, not returning to England until 1806. Despite his detainment, the transportation of the crates continued piecemeal until 1815 when the last crates were taken to England, most on Royal Navy ships with some on government owned vessels.

Had he been quicker packing, or Napoleon slower in mobilising, it could very well have been Nelson bringing the Marbles, and the other items, to England stored in the holds of his fleet.

Article on the 2015/2016 expedition to the wreck of the Mentor: http://tiny.cc/8g4bkz *(Kytherian Research Group, pictured above)*

The Anglo-French Wars over Antiquities: http://tiny.cc/6i4bkz

AJN

HOW MANY GUNS?

This is not a correction per se, but in Issue #3 we talked about the *USS Constitution* having 54 guns. A couple of people have commented on this, stating that she was configured with 44 guns, but it is important to note that the loadout of guns on a ship could change during its lifetime.

For example, when launched in 1765, *HMS Victory* was built for 100 guns. In 1799, when she was pressed back into service after being used for a few years as a hospital ship, she was re-configured for 104 guns, which is the number she carried at Trafalgar in 1805 (yes, we are ignoring the 18lb she carried for use in her launch).

So, when we state the number of guns for a ship, we try to do it for the specific time we are writing about, but please let us know if you disagree.

AJN

USS CONSTITUTTON

USS Constitution, nicknamed 'Old Ironsides', is a 44 gun heavy frigate of the United States Navy and is currently berthed in Boston as a museum ship. She is the oldest commissioned warship in the world still afloat, having been launched in 1797. Constitution is perhaps best known for her battles with various British vessels during the war of 1812.

The ship was built at Edmund Hartt's shipyard in the north of Boston, and was one of six frigates authorised by the Naval Act of 1794. After two failed attempts in late September 1797, Constitution was launched on the 21st October 1797. Her armament initially consisted of thirty 24 pounder long guns, twenty 32 pounder Carronades and two 24 pounder bow chasers.

She spent her early years as the flagship of the early US Navy's West Indies and Mediterranean squadrons, spending a brief period in ordinary between 1801-1803. It was during the war of 1812 that Constitution etched her name into the annals of history, coming out the victor in a number of skirmishes with vessels of the Royal Navy. Perhaps the most famous of these battles came against the British frigates HMS Guerriere on 29th August 1812 and HMS Java on 29th December of the same year. During both of these actions, Constitution managed to overpower her adversaries, eventually damaging the British ships so badly that the crews burnt them rather allow capture. It has been said that as a result of the actions of Constitution and her fellow heavy frigates, the British Admiralty ordered its vessels not to challenge American ships one-on-one. It was during this period that the ship also received its nickname, 'Old Ironsides', as the shot of the British ships seemed to have little effect, bouncing off of Constitution's thick wooden hull.

Following the war of 1812, Constitution spent another period laid up in ordinary before spending several years as part of the Mediterranean squadron. She was converted to a school ship in 1860 and was then restored to her 1812 configuration in 1906-1907 in Boston. The ship underwent several rounds of restoration and conservation during the twentieth century, before finally sailing under her own power once again on 21st July 1997, the first time the ship had done so in 116 years.

Today, USS Constitution operates with a small US Navy crew, who perform ceremonial duties and provide free guided tours to the public. She is berthed at Pier One of the old Charlestown Navy Yard, near a privately run museum dedicated to the ship. Once a year, the ship undertakes a turnaround cruise, during which the ship is towed out into the harbour and turned around, ensuring the vessel weathers evenly.

AV

BOOK: GIBRALTAR AS A NAVAL BASE AND DOCKYARD: VOLUME 2

£3.99 87 PAGES PAPERBACK (KINDLE VERSION ALSO AVAILABLE)

The Naval Dockyards Society (who we will talk about more in the next issue) have just released a updated publication on the Gibraltar dockyards. This is a reprint of the papers from the 2004 conference, and covers Gibraltar from 1600 up to the mid 20th Century.

There are eight papers in this publication, all with detailed references for the scholars amongst you. The papers cover the importance of Gibraltar to the Royal Navy, the sieges in 1726 and 1779, the role it played in supplying Nelson and the Mediterranean fleet, and more.

Gibraltar has had many '*rulers*', from the Phoenicians and Romans, to the Moors, to the Spanish, and currently to the British, and if you want to get a real feel for the importance of Gibraltar for the Royal Navy over the centuries, then this is the material for you.

We would say this publication is aimed at the hard-core enthusiast or researcher, and the tables and references included are invaluable for further investigation, but everyone will glean some gems from this with some dedicated reading.

https://www.amazon.co.uk/Gibraltar-Naval-Base-Dockyard-Transactions-ebook/dp/B07K5C7R2L

AJN

GAME: CLEAR THE DECKS!

Crispy Games Co. £29.99 (£4.99 for a player mat) 1-4 Players

https://www.crispygamesco.com/ UK: http://tiny.cc/dwt7iz (when shipping allows)

We stumbled across this board game, which is relatively new, and are delighted that we did. It is for 1 to 4 players, and uses a card deck for player actions and a card deck for the actions of the ship you are fighting. The larger the opponent, the more guns and crew it can bring to bear and you have to work with your teammates to take it out. You have to work through a stack of cards in each key location until you punch holes through its hull.

It sounds remarkably simple, but we soon found out that if you fire the three guns under your control in one turn, the next turn you won't be able to fire as they are re-loading (unless you have a crew or tactics card that aids you). Also, it is no good just shooting everything in sight; it is not always guns that appear on the enemy ship, there are items such as rigging and enemy crew that have to be removed. This leads to planning with your team, so there are a good deal of tactics involved.

Inside the manual, there are set-up instructions for nine different classes of ship (cutter, 15 guns, up to frigate, 45 guns) and for the number of players in your team, and once you have played it to familiarise yourself with the rules, the game plays well, with each turn running quickly.

Situations can appear dire at times, but with careful shooting (such as taking the guns out but leaving the rigging, giving you a chance to get useful cards that can repair your own damage), you can turn the battle around. The different types of targets take different types of ammo, so this adds another layer of complexity.

Though this game may look simplistic at first glance, it really encourages teamwork and strategy. We do recommend spending additional money to buy the extra play mats as these really enhance the playing experience. There are a couple of blank cards included, so you can create your own items, which is nice: we are thinking of a carronade card (or two).

And make sure you shuffle the decks really, really, well before starting play. We have to go now, we have a score to settle with a frigate...

AJN and AV

Where did Napoleon hide his armies?
Up his sleevies...

DID YOU MISS?: THE SIX FRIGATES

One book we've had recommended to us many times over the past few years is *The Six Frigates*, by Ian W. Toll. This was published in 2008, and does not appear to be available in print at the moment, so we had to turn to eBay to source a printed copy (no electronic version available either at this time).

After finally sourcing our copy, we settled down to the 500+ pages with some eagerness, and we were not disappointed. The book charts the creation of the U.S. Navy, building to a climax of the War of 1812.

In particular, as with the title, it focuses on the six frigates ordered to be built by President John Adams. The frigates (*USS United States, USS Constellation, USS Congress, USS Chesapeake, USS President, and USS Constitution*) are central to the narrative but the author tells this more like an adventure than a history book, even though it has an extensive Bibliography and source-notes.

The research and detail in this book is impressive, and has many excerpts and quotes taken directly from ship's logs and government papers. The book not only covers the ships and the battles they fought, but also describes the pressures on the sailors themselves, both political and personal, and brings life at sea up close and personal.

Some of the numbers quoted feel a little dated now, there has been a lot more research and analysis on the various battles as to the casualties on all sides, but highly recommended nonetheless, if you can find a copy.

AJN

VIRTUAL VISITS

With travel restrictions in place all at the moment, you can still get a virtual museum fix of some online collections (please note that the *Age of Sail* link to these is tenuous, but we thought they may be of interest).

HMB Endeavour

A virtual tour of the replica of the *Endeavour*.

17th Century Shipwreck

A virtual dive on the wreck of the Dutch merchant vessel *Melckmeyt*.

HMS Surprise Replica

A video walkthrough of the replica HMS Surprise.

Imperial War Museum, HMS Belfast

A virtual tour of *HMS Belfast*, the WWII light cruiser.

AJN

The Carronade, often nicknamed 'the smasher', was a short-range naval artillery piece favoured by the Royal Navy in the late eighteenth and early nineteenth centuries. Capable of firing a large shot, requiring only a small amount of powder and half the crew of a long naval gun, Carronades were a highly effective option for causing damage to enemy ships at point blank range. The invention of the Carronade has been credited mainly to two men, General Robert Melville and Sir Charles Gascoigne, and they were produced by the Carron Company; an ironworks in Falkirk, Scotland, based on the river Carron.

The first recorded use of a Carronade on a Royal Navy ship was in 1779, and by 1781 around 400 ships had been armed with the weapon. The Royal Navy used a variety of different sized Carronades, ranging from 12 pounders up to 68 pounders. These 68 pounders were among the heaviest naval ordnance used at the time, with two being fitted to *HMS Victory's* forecastle. One of the first shots that Victory fired during the battle of Trafalgar came from her port Carronade, which was loaded with a single 68 pound round shot along with a keg of 500 musket balls. This cannister in particular wreaked havoc on the deck of the French flagship *Bucentaure*, cutting down scores of sailors.

The advantages of using Carronades came with their low usage of powder and crew. For example, a 68 pounder required a charge of only 5½ pounds of gunpowder and a crew of just five men. When compared to a 32 pounder long gun, which needed a full charge of 10 pounds of gunpowder and a gun crew of fourteen men, it is easy to see the benefits. Another unique feature of the Carronade was the low velocity of the projectile when fired. This meant that while shots did not always pass directly through the hull of an enemy ship, it would create an ugly hole that would not only be difficult to fix, but would also throw out a large amount of splinters. The Carronade was also among the first naval weapons to be fitted with a disport sight, enabling gun captains to sight the gun using its true bore line, leading to increased accuracy. Furthermore, Carronades were designed so that the shot loaded would have only a small amount of windage, the space between the shot and the barrel of the gun, leading to a slightly better flight path for the shot.

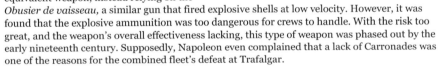

Carronades were mounted on both regular wheeled carriages and on sliding carriages, such as those found on Victory's forecastle. Elevation could be achieved through a screw at the rear of the gun, removing the need for a quoin. Despite this, the replica Carronades on *HMS Victory* (see right) are curiously displayed with a quoin in place, with the elevating screw not present.

The French navy was slow to produce an equivalent weapon, instead relying on the *Obusier de vaisseau,* a similar gun that fired explosive shells at low velocity. However, it was found that the explosive ammunition was too dangerous for crews to handle. With the risk too great, and the weapon's overall effectiveness lacking, this type of weapon was phased out by the early nineteenth century. Supposedly, Napoleon even complained that a lack of Carronades was one of the reasons for the combined fleet's defeat at Trafalgar.

The Carronade was introduced to the US Navy in the early nineteenth century. Henry Foxall, superintendent of the Eagle foundry in Philadelphia was responsible for overseeing the casting of thee first American Carronades, the largest of which were 42 pounders. *USS Constitution's* Carronades in particular were highly effective in her skirmishes with *HMS Guerriere* and *HMS Java*, making short work of both British frigates' forces. Records even show references to *Constitution* having 'Carronades' in her fighting tops early on in her serving career. However, in reality, it is likely that these weapons mounted in the tops were light howitzer type guns, similar to the French *Obusier de vaisseau*.

While best used in tandem with long guns, several ships throughout the period were fitted with an experimental load out of exclusively Carronades. An example of this was the British ship *HMS Glatton*, a 56 gun fourth-rate ship, acquired from the East India Company in 1795. *Glatton* was given an armament of twenty eight 32 pounder Carronades on her upper deck and twenty eight 68 pounder Carronades on her lower deck. It was in this configuration that *Glatton*, then under the command of Captain William Bligh of *Bounty* infamy, took part in the battle of Copenhagen in 1801. Where this configuration worked for *Glatton* during this close-quarters conflict, other ships fitted exclusively with Carronades did not fare as well. The problem being that an enemy vessel fitted with long guns could simply stay out of range of the ship's Carronades, while attacking with her long guns. An example of this came during the action between *HMS Phoebe* and *USS Essex*, where the British ship gained victory using this tactic.

Although devastating up close, the Carronade could never replace the long gun. Nevertheless, Carronades were widely used by both the Royal Navy and US Navy throughout the early nineteenth century, until the weapon was phased out due to the advent of rifled, shell-firing guns.

AV

TRAFALGAR SHIPS 003: HMS AGAMEMNON

HMS Agamemnon: sixty-four guns of third-rate ship-of-the-line and a favourite of Nelson, was launched at Buckler's Hard in 1781. Nelson did not command her until 1793, but in her twenty-eight years of service she saw the likes of Benjamin Caldwell, Samuel Hood, John Harvey, and Robert Fancourt command her. Her design was that of the Ardent class, and her designer, Robert Slade, is the same man who had earlier designed *HMS Victory (1765)*.

Along with her battle honours (Ushant 1781, The Saints 1782, Genoa 1795, Copenhagen 1801, Trafalgar 1805, and San Domingo 1806), she also had the dubious honour of running aground three times. Firstly, in 1800 when she hit Penmarks Rocks (north of Lorient, France). Secondly, during the Battle of Copenhagen (1801), when along with two other ships she was pulled free during the night, and finally on June 16th, 1809, in Maldonado Bay by the River Plate. This third time proved fatal for her,

Harold Wyllie etching of HMS Agamemnon , off Portsmouth in 1781.

and she was stripped by the other ships in the squadron, though it is worth noting she was in a poor state of repair already by this time. To add a little more to her chequered career, her crew mutinied in 1797 at the Nore.

Under Nelson, who commanded her for three years from 1793, she blockaded Toulon, chased the French *Melpomène (1794, 38 guns)* - but failed to catch her. Her troops, led by Nelson, captured Bastia, Corsica (1794), and took part in the siege of Calvi, where Nelson lost the sight in his right eye. At the Battle of Genoa (1795), the *Agamemnon* spent some three-and-a-half hours battling the 80 gun *Ça Ira*, which was eventually captured.

Nelson was promoted to Commodore in 1796, and on June 10th of that year he transferred his flag to *HMS Captain (1787, 75 guns)*, whilst the *Agamemnon* went off for another refit (one of many during her lifetime).

As often with British crews, the name Agamemnon proved to be a bit of a mouthful for them, so they nicknamed her the *'eggs-and-bacon'*.

AJN

Why couldn't the pirates play cards?
Because the Captain was standing on the deck...

SET SAIL FOR DESOLATION ISLAND!

This reviewer heartily recommends this novel by the formidable Patrick O'Brian – one of the finest writers of naval fiction. Desolation Island is the fifth in a series of twenty-two novels in what is known as the Aubrey-Maturin series, written over about twenty-five years. You can read the Aubrey-Maturin books as stand-alone novels, but for those who are interested, the first book is *Master and Commander*, made famous by the 2005 film.

Desolation Island begins in England around 1809, shortly after the Royal Navy's successful campaign on Mauritius. Our hero, Captain Jack Aubrey is preparing to set sail to Australia onboard *HMS Leopard*, a fourth-rate which carries some civilian convicts, including women. O'Brian takes us aboard the *Leopard* at Portsmouth, around the Cape of Good Hope, and into the Pacific as we join Aubrey *et al* on an epic voyage. The descriptions of naval life are a real highlight - you can almost feel the motion of the ship as she battles storms, sense the hardship of men working the bilge pumps, and feel their fear as they encounter the enemy.

The characters likewise are described in great detail. Aubrey is a tough, experienced captain with a lively sense of humour, who enjoys re-telling meeting Lord Nelson over dinner. Next, we have his best friend, Doctor Stephen Maturin. Maturin appears a reserved but highly intelligent gentleman, praised in the medical profession and with a passion for flora and fauna.

O'Brian pays great attention to the language his characters use, which makes the story more credible. He also uses quite a bit of humour, which gives a lighter tone than some historical novels this reviewer has read.

One possible caveat is the rather detailed inclusion of maritime terms – for example, luffing up, gammoning and so forth. However, you should be able to follow the story easily enough, even if you allow a few terms to wash over you!

There is also a helpful sketch of a square-rigged ship showing its masts and principle sails. Although the *Leopard* was a fourth-rate (between 46 and 60 guns), her main features were much the same as those found on larger ships such as *HMS Victory*. In conclusion, Desolation Island is an exciting adventure yarn, with memorable characters, but be prepared for some technical language!

A CALL FOR INFORMATION...

Last month, we were asked why the Royal Navy lower the flags at sunset, in the ceremony known as hauling down the colours.

To be honest, there was some head-scratching, and we knew that answering *'because they've always done that'* was not good enough.

We spoke to some navy personnel, and they could not give us an answer, and we did some research and have not found anything definite as to when it started and why.

We had the responses of *'well, they can't be seen at night, so why fly the flag?'*, but the most intriguing one concerns Gibraltar.

One of our colleagues has heard the tale that when Gibraltar was ceded to the British in 1713, the Queen of Spain (Maria Luisa of Savoy, wife of Philip V), said she would never sleep whilst the British flag flew over Gibraltar.

Respectful of any royal, the British navy decided to lower the flag every sunset to allow the queen to sleep.

We love this story, and we absolutely hope that it is true, but unfortunately we have found no records or evidence that this is the case.

So if you, our readers, can shed any light on either the tale, or another reason (even should it be so boring as the flag cannot be seen at night), then please get in touch.

traftimes@gmail.com

AJN

THE TRAFALGAR TIMES

The Trafalgar Times is a publication put together to share information primarily focusing on navies and events around the time of the Battle of Trafalgar. This scope, however, is not limited, and we aim to cover media and events that may appeal to anyone who has an interest in the age of sail.

If you have any suggestions, article submissions, or corrections, then please email us:
traftimes@gmail.com

 @traftimes

HET SHEEPVART, AMSTERDAM

Housed in the old arsenal (dating from 1656), the Dutch National Maritime Museum is a thoroughly enjoyable experience.

Not as busy as the Rijksmuseum, the Stedelijk, or the Van Gogh museums, this spacious and well laid out attraction also has three ships (two afloat) to visit. On our visit, we spent six hours there and that was without seeing the outside ships as the weather had forced them to close the jetty. The tickets (€16.00) include an audio guide with 11 different languages available.

The building itself is divided into three wings by compass point, with the East wing holding maps, yacht models, figureheads, and navigational instruments. The West wing covers the 'Golden Age' (17th Century), whales and whaling, and an activity for young people showing how life has changed onboard ships since the 17th Century. The North wing has a section on polar exploration and a large focus on the Dutch navy in the 17th and 18th centuries. Of the outside ships, in pride of place is the replica of the 1749 Dutch East Indiaman, the Amsterdam (right), which we hope to return to when it is open to review.

There are many stunning models on display, and the audio guide and descriptive text is pretty good. The thing we felt it lacked most was there was very little on actual ship-building techniques and materials, which is an important part of the story.

But, it is a gorgeous building, you have plenty of space to roam and inspect, and the café food was poshed up nicely as well. Just check the weather when you plan to go in case the jetty and ships are closed.

https://www.hetscheepvaartmuseum.com/

AJN

> *Why don't people name their kids Napoleon anymore?*
> *It's too complex...*

SAILING LIKE COLUMBUS

We've had a busy quarter, travel-wise, and our highlight has to be the 3 hour cruise on the replica of the Christopher Columbus ship, the *"Nau Santa Maria",* sailing from Funchal, Madeira. Unfortunately it was purely under motor power rather than sail, but it was a very pleasant way to spend our first morning there.

The ship takes up to 40 people, and when full it does not feel cramped, and you get a free sampler of Madeira wine and a slice of honey-cake to help you survive the "rigours" of the voyage. Only 30 minutes into our journey we were joined by dolphins who played in our bow-wake for some time. The crew point out highlights as you sail along the coastline, and there is a bar area and toilets should you require them. The bar has some interesting oddities stuck to the walls (think Quint's place from *Jaws*).

This is definitely a more tourist-biased trip than a historical or sailing experience, but for 35 Euros it is not too expensive, especially as a dolphin watching trip alone costs a similar price. Our top tip would be to get up into the prow—you can cross over the bits there to lean out over the side, perfect for when/if the dolphins join you.

NB—We went on the morning trip, but we saw her with her mainsails out on the afternoon trip, so we hope you have a good wind to experience that. Also, we booked in advance through Expedia, saving 5 Euros. www.santamariadecolombo.com

AJN

APPENDICES:

Map of Cadiz/Trafalgar/Gibraltar Area

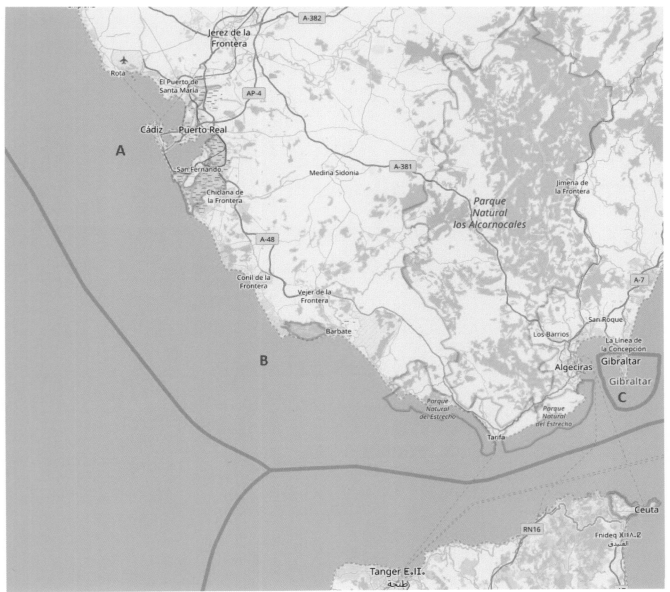

© OpenStreetMap contributors

A—Cadiz

B—Cape Trafalgar

C—Gibraltar

Nelson's Memorandum *(Part 1)*

Victory, off Cadiz, 9th October, 1805

Memn.

Thinking it almost impossible to bring a Fleet of forty Sail of the Line into a Line of Battle in variable winds, thick weather, and other circumstances which must occur, without such a loss of time that the opportunity would probably be lost of bringing the Enemy to Battle in such a manner as to make the business decisive.

I have therefore made up my mind to keep the Fleet in that position of sailing (with the exception of the First and Second in Command) that the Order of Sailing is to be the Order of Battle, placing the Fleet in two Lines of sixteen Ships each, with an Advanced Squadron of eight of the fastest sailing Two-decked Ships, which will always make, if wanted, a line of twenty-four Sail, on whichever Line the Commander in Chief may direct.

The Second in Command will, after my intentions are made known to him, have the entire direction of his Line to make the attack upon the Enemy, and to follow up the blow until they are captured or destroyed.

If the Enemy's Fleet should be seen to windward in Line of Battle, and that the two Lines and the Advanced Squadron can fetch them, they will probably be so extended that their Van could not succour their friends.

I should therefore probably make the Second in Command's signal to lead through, about their twelfth Ship from their Rear, (or wherever he could fetch, if not able to get so far advanced); my Line would lead through about their Centre, and the Advanced Squadron to cut two or three or four Ships a-head of their Centre, so as to ensure getting at their Commander-in-Chief, on whom every effort must be made to capture.

The whole impression of the British Fleet must be to overpower from two or three Ships a-head of their Commander-in-Chief, supposed to be in the Centre, to the Rear of their Fleet. I will suppose twenty Sail of the Enemy's Line to be untouched, it must be some time before they could perform a manoeuvre to bring their force compact to attack any part of the British Fleet engaged, or to succour their own Ships, which indeed would be impossible without mixing with the Ships engaged. Something must be left to chance; nothing is sure in a Sea Fight beyond all others. Shot will carry away the masts and yards of friends as well as foes; but I look with confidence to a Victory before the Van of the Enemy could succour their Rear, and then that the British Fleet would most of them be ready to receive their twenty Sail of the Line, or to pursue them, should they endeavour to make off.

If the Van of the Enemy tacks, the Captured Ships must run to leeward of the British Fleet; if the Enemy wears, the British must place themselves between the Enemy and the Captured, and disabled British Ships; and should the Enemy close, I have no fears as to the result.

(Continued)

Nelson's Memorandum *(Part 2)*

Victory, off Cadiz, 9th October, 1805

Memn.

(continued)

The Second in Command will in all possible things direct the movements of his Line, by keeping them as compact as the nature of the circumstances will admit. Captains are to look to their particular Line as their rallying point. But, in case Signals can neither be seen or perfectly understood, no Captain can do very wrong if he places his Ship alongside that of an Enemy.

Of the intended attack from to windward, the Enemy in Line of Battle ready to receive an attack.

The divisions of the British Fleet will be brought nearly within gun shot of the Enemy's Centre. The signal will most probably then be made for the Lee Line to bear up together, to set all their sails, even steering sails, in order to get as quickly as possible to the Enemy's Line, and to cut through, beginning from the 12 Ship from the Enemy's Rear. Some Ships may not get through their exact place, but they will always be at hand to assist their friends; and if any are thrown round the Rear of the Enemy, they will effectually complete the business of twelve Sail of the Enemy. Should the Enemy wear together, or bear up and sail large, still the twelve Ships composing, in the first position, the Enemy's Rear, are to be the object of attack of the Lee Line, unless otherwise directed from the Commander-in-Chief which is scarcely to be expected as the entire management of the Lee Line, after the intentions of the Commander-in-Chief, is [are] signified, is intended to be left to the judgment of the Admiral commanding that Line.

The remainder of the Enemy's Fleet, 34 Sail, are to be left to the management of the Commander-in-Chief, who will endeavour to take care that the movements of the Second in Command are as little interrupted as is possible.

NELSON AND BRONTE .

Nelson, by John Francis Rigaud, 1781

Printed in the London Gazette, 1805. Note HMS Africa off station!

Collingwood's First Despatch *(Part 1)*

This is the first despatch, after Trafalgar, that Collingwood sent back to England with Captain Lapenotière aboard HMS Pickle. This despatch arrived at the Admiralty on November 6th, 15 days after being sent. The next news did not arrive with the Admiralty in England until November 15th.

To William Marsden Esq., Admiralty, London

Euryalus, off Cape Trafalgar, Oct. 22.

Sir,

The ever to be lamented death of Vice Admiral Lord Viscount Nelson, who, in the late conflict with the enemy, fell in the hour of victory, leaves to me the duty of informing my Lord Commissioners of the Admiralty, that on the 19th inst. it was communicated to the Commander in Chief from the ships watching the motions of the enemy in Cadiz, that the combined fleet had put to sea; as they sailed with light winds westerly, his Lordship concluded their destination was the Mediterranean, and immediately made all sail for the Streights' entrance, with the British squadron, consisting of twenty-seven ships, three of them sixty-fours, where his Lordship was informed by Captain Blackwood (whose vigilance in watching, and giving notice of the enemy's movements, has been highly meritorious) that they had not yet passed the Streights.

On Monday, the 21st instant, at day light, when Cape Trafalgar bore E. by S. about seven leagues, the enemy was discovered six or seven miles to the eastward, the wind about west, and very light, the Commander in Chief immediately made the signal for the fleet to bear up in two columns, as they are formed in order of sailing; a mode of attack his Lordship had previously directed, to avoid the inconvenience and delay in forming a line of battle in the usual manner. The enemy's line consisted of thirty-three ships (of which 18 were French and 15 Spanish) commanded in chief by Admiral Villeneuve; the Spaniards under the direction of Gravina, wore, with their heads to the northward, and formed the line of battle with great closeness and correctness;-but as the mode of attack was unusual, so the structure of their line was new; it formed a crescent convexing to leeward-so that, in leading down to their centre, I had both their van and rear, abaft the beam; before the fire opened, every alternate ship was about a cable's length to windward of her second a-head, and a-stern, forming a kind of double line, and appeared, when on their beam, to leave a very littler interval between them; and this without crowding their ships. Admiral Villeneuve was in the Bucentaure in the centre, and the Prince of Asturias bore Gravina's flag in the rear; but the French and Spanish ships were mixed without any apparent regard to order of national squadron.

As the mode of our attack had been previously determined on, and communicated to the Flag Officers and Captains, few signals were necessary, and none were made, except to direct close order as the lines bore down. The Commander in Chief in the Victory led the weather column, and the Royal Sovereign, which bore my flag, the lee.

The action began at twelve o'clock, by the leading ships of the columns breaking through the enemy's line, the Commander in Chief about the tenth ship from the van, the Second in Command about the twelfth from the rear, leaving the van of the enemy unoccupied; the succeeding ships breaking through, in all parts, astern of their leaders, and engaging the enemy at the muzzles of their guns: the conflict was severe; the enemy's ships were fought with a gallantry highly honourable to their officers, but the attack on them was irresistible, and it pleased the Almighty Disposer of all Events, to grant his Majesty's arms a complete and glorious victory.

Collingwood's First Despatch *(Part 2)*

(continued)

About three P.M. many of the enemy's ships having struck their colours, their line gave way: Admiral Gravina, with ten ships, joining their frigates to leeward, stood towards Cadiz. The five headmost ships in their van tacked, and standing to the southward, to windward, of the British line, were engaged, and the sternmost of them taken:- the others went off, leaving to his Majesty's squadron, nineteen ships of the line, (of which two are first-rates, the Santissima Trinidad and the Santa Anna) with three Flag Officers, viz. Admiral Villeneuve, the Commander in Chief, Don Ignatio Maria D'Aliva, Vice Admiral, and the Spanish Rear Admiral Don Baltazar Hidalgo Cisneros.

After such a victory it may appear unnecessary to enter into encomiums on the particular parts taken by the several Commanders; the conclusion says more on the subject than I have language to express; the spirit which animated all was the same; when all exerted themselves zealously in their country's service, all deserve that their high merits should stand recorded; and never was high merit more conspicuous than in the battle I have described.

The Achille (a French 74), after having surrendered, by some mismanagement of the Frenchmen took fire and blew up; two hundred of her men were saved by the tenders.

A circumstance occurred during the action, which so strongly marks the invincible spirit of British seamen, when engaging the enemies of their country, that I cannot resist the pleasure I have in making it known to their Lordships; the Temeraire was boarded by accident, or design, by a French ship on one side, and a Spaniard on the other; the contest was vigorous, but, in the end, the combined ensigns were torn from the poop, and the British hoisted in their places.

Such a battle could not be fought without sustaining a great loss of men. I have not only to lament in common with the British Navy, and the British Nation, in the fall of the Commander in Chief, the loss of a Hero, whose name will be immortal, and his memory ever dear to his country; but my heart is rent with the most poignant grief for the death of a friend, to whom, by many years intimacy, and a perfect knowledge of the virtues of his mind, which inspired ideas superior to the common race of men, I was bound by the strongest ties of affection; a grief to which even the glorious occasion in which he fell, does not bring the consolation which perhaps it ought; his Lordship received a musket ball in his left breast, about the middle of the action, and sent an officer to me immediately with his last farewell; and soon after expired.

I have also to lament the loss of those excellent officers, Captains Duff, of the Mars, and Cooke, of the Bellerophon; I have yet heard of no others.

I fear the numbers that have fallen will be found very great, when the returns come to me; but it having blown a gale of wind ever since the action, I have not yet had it in my power to collect any reports from the ships.

The Royal Sovereign having lost her masts, except the tottering foremast, I called the Euryalus to me, which the action continued, which ship lying within hail, made my signals, a service Captain Blackwood performed with great attention; after the action, I shifted my flag to her, that I might more easily communicate my orders to, and collect the ships, and towed the Royal Sovereign out to seaward. The whole fleet were now in a very perilous situation, many dismasted, all shattered, in thirteen fathom water, off the Shoals of Trafalgar, and when I made the signal to prepare to anchor, few of the ships had an anchor to let go, their cables being shot; but the same good Providence which aided us through such a day, preserved us in the night, by the wind shifting a few points, and drifting the ships off the land.

Having thus detailed the proceedings of the fleet on this occasion, I beg to congratulate their Lordships on a victory, which, I hope will add a ray to the glory of his Majesty's Crown, and be attended with public benefit to our country.

I am,

C. Collingwood

Collingwood's Second Despatch

This is the second despatch Collingwood sent back to England. This was taken from the Euryalus (Collingwood's temporary flagship) by HMS Entrepenante to Faro, Portugal. Via the British Embassy in Lisbon it was bought to England onboard the packet Lord Walsingham. It arrived with the Admiralty 11 days after the first despatch.

Euryalus, off Cadiz, Oct 24, 1805

SIR,

In my letter of 22nd, I detailed to you, for the information of my Lords Commissioners of the Admiralty, the proceedings of his Majesty's squadron on the day of the action, and that proceeding it, since which I have had a continued series of misfortunes; but they are of a kind that human prudence could not possibly provide against, or my skill prevent.

On the 22nd, in the morning, a strong southerly wind blew, with squally weather, which, however, did not prevent the activity of the Officers and Seamen of such ships as were manageable, from getting hold of many of the prizes (thirteen or fourteen), and towing them off to the westward, where I ordered them to rendezvous round the Royal Sovereign, in tow by the Neptune: but on the 23rd the gale increased, and the sea ran so high that many of them broke the tow rope, and drifted far to leeward before they were got hold of again; and some of them, taking advantage of the dark and boisterous night, got before the wind, and have, perhaps, drifted upon the shore and sunk; on the afternoon of that day the remnant of the Combined Fleet, ten sail of ships, who had not been much engaged, stood up to leeward of my shattered and straggled charge, as if meaning to attack them, which obliged me to collect a force out of the least injured ships, and form to leeward for their defence; all this retarded the progress of the hulks, and the bad weather continuing, determined me to destroy all the leewardmost that could be cleared of the men, considering that keeping possession of the ships was a matter of little consequence, compared with the chance of their falling again into the hands of the enemy; but even this was an arduous task in the high sea which was running. I hope, however, it has been accomplished to a considerable extent; I entrusted it to skilful officers, who would spare no pains to execute what was possible. The Captains of the Prince and Neptune cleared the Trinidad and sunk her. Captains Hope, Bayntun, and. Malcolm, who joined the fleet this moment from Gibraltar, had the charge of destroying the four others. The Redoubtable sunk astern of the Swiftsure while in tow. The Santa Anna, I have no doubt, is sunk, as her side was almost beat in; and such is the shattered condition of the whole of them, that unless the weather moderates I doubt whether I shall be able to carry a ship of them into port. I hope their Lordships will approve of what I (having only in consideration the destruction of the enemy's fleet) have thought a measure of absolute necessity.

Have taken Admiral Villeneuve into this ship; Vice Admiral Don Aliva is dead. Whenever the temper of the weather will permit, and I can spare a frigate (for there were only four in the action with the fleet, Euryalus, Sirius, Phoebe, and Naiad; the Melpomene joined the 22nd, and the Eurydice and Scout the 23rd) I shall collect the other flag officers, and send them to England, with their flags, (if they do not all go to the bottom), to be laid at his Majesty's feet.

There were four thousand troops embarked, under the command of General Contamin, who was taken with Admiral Villeneuve in the Bucentaure.

I am,

C. Collingwood

Last Letters

Nelson's Last Letter to Emma Hamilton:

'Victory', October 19, 1805, Noon

Cadiz, E.S.E. 16 Leagues

My dearest beloved Emma, the dear friend of my bosom,

The signal has been made that the enemy's combined fleet are coming out of Port. We have very little wind, so that I have no hopes of seeing them before tomorrow. May the God of Battles crown my endeavours with success; at all events, I will take care that my name shall ever be most dear to you and Horatia, both of whom I love as much as my own life. And as my last writing before the Battle will be to you, so I hope in God that I shall live to finish my letter after the Battle.

May heaven bless you prayers, your

NELSON AND BRONTE

October 20th - In the morning we were close to the mouth of the Straits, but the wind had not come far enough to the westward to allow the Combined Fleets to weather the Shoals off Trafalgar; but they were counted as far as forty Sail of Ships of War, which I suppose to be thirty-four of the Line, and six Frigates. A group of them was seen off the Lighthouse of Cadiz this morning, but it blows so very fresh and thick weather, that I rather believe they will go into the Harbour before night. May God Almighty give us success over these fellows, and enable us to get a Peace ....

Nelson's Last Letter to his daughter, Horatia:

'Victory', October 19, 1805

My dearest angel,

I was made happy by the pleasure of receiving your letter of September 19, and I rejoice my dear Lady Hamilton, who most dearly loves you. Give her a kiss for me. The Combined Fleets of the enemy are now reported to be coming out of Cadiz, and therefore, I answer your letter, my dearest Horatia, to mark to you that you are ever uppermost in my thoughts. I shall be sure of your prayers for my safety, conquest, and speedy return to dear Merton and our dearest good Lady Hamilton. Be a good girl; mind what Miss Connor says to you.

Receive, my dearest Horatia, the affectionate parental blessing of your father,

NELSON AND BRONTE

The Trafalgar Woods

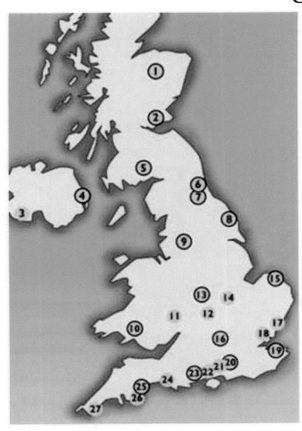

1. Defence — Moray
2. Swiftsure — Perth & Kinross
3. Belleisle — Fermanagh
4. Dreadnought — N. Down
5. Defiance — Dumfries & Galloway
6. Royal Sovereign — Northumberland
7. Ajax — Durham
8. Revenge — North Yorkshire
9. Polyphemus — Lancashire
10. Spartiate — Carmarthenshire
11. Colossus — Herefordshire
12. Mars — Warwickshire
13. Achilles — Derbyshire
14. Leviathan — Leicestershire
15. Tonnant — Norfolk
16. Neptune — Oxfordshire
17. Prince — Suffolk
18. Bellerophon — Essex
19. Victory — Kent
20. Orion — Hampshire
21. Thunderer — Berkshire
22. Temeraire — Hampshire
23. Agamemnon — Hampshire
24. Africa — Dorset
25. Conqueror — Devon
26. Britannia — Devon
27. Minotaur — Cornwall

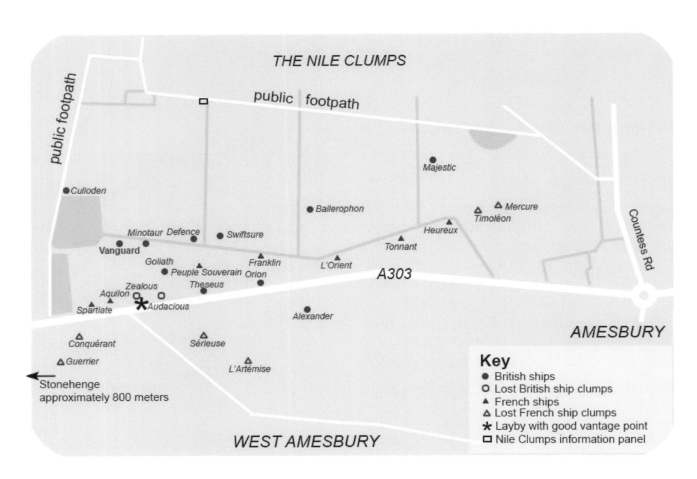

Heart of Oak Original Lyrics

Come, cheer up, my lads, 'tis to glory we steer,

To add something more to this wonderful year;

To honour we call you, as freemen not slaves,

For who are so free as the sons of the waves?

Heart of Oak are our ships,

Jolly Tars are our men,

We always are ready: Steady, boys, Steady!

We'll fight and we'll conquer again and again.

We ne'er see our foes but we wish them to stay,

They never see us but they wish us away;

If they run, why we follow, and run them ashore,

For if they won't fight us, what can we do more?

Heart of Oak are our ships,

Jolly Tars are our men,

We always are ready: Steady, boys, Steady!

We'll fight and we'll conquer again and again.

Britannia triumphant her ships rule the seas,

Her watch word is 'Justice' her password is 'Free',

So come cheer up my lads, with one heart let us sing,

Our soldiers, our sailors, our statesmen, our king

Heart of Oak are our ships,

Jolly Tars are our men,

We always are ready: Steady, boys, Steady!

We'll fight and we'll conquer again and again.

'Heart of Oak' was composed by William Boyce (1711-1779), and is the official anthem of the Royal Navy of the United Kingdom. The original words were written by David Garrick (1717-1779), and the whole piece was assembled in 1759, being first performed in public in 1760.

In 1809, a revised version was released, with amended lyrics by the Reverend Rylance. (there are also alternative words for the first and last choruses which have been released). The lyrics above are those of the original, 1759, version.

https://www.youtube.com/watch?v=4NXFCDgyanA

Horatio Nelson's Family Tree

Are you doing your family tree research, hoping for a link to a Nelson, a Collingwood, a Villeneuve or even a John Paul Jones? Well, here are some of Nelson's ancestors, maybe you can find yourself a link to his tree?

(Source: Wikitree)

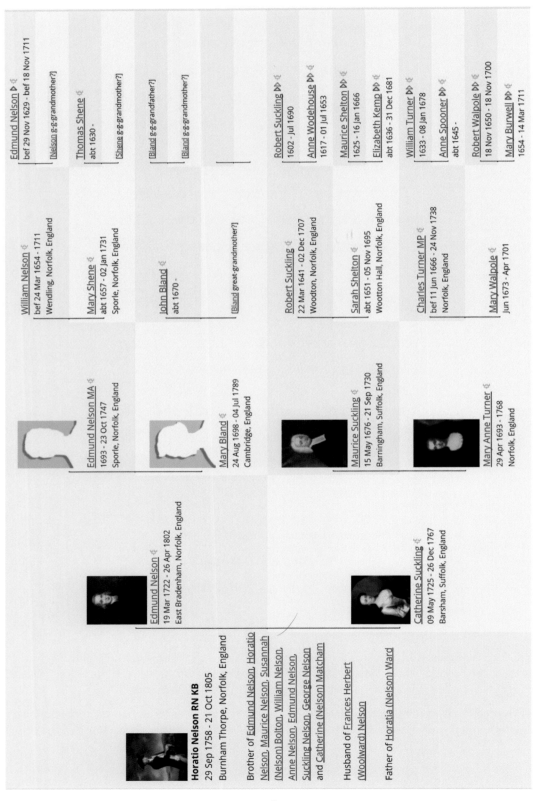

Casabianca: On the Burning Deck

In 1826, nearly thirty years after the Battle of the Nile, Felicia Hemans published her poem 'Casabianca'. The poem relates the story of the son of Louis de Casabianca as he stayed at his post on the *L'Orient* as it burned, before exploding. Many of us are aware of the poem, but you may not have known the context or that it was written by a British poet.

The boy stood on the burning deck,
Whence all but he had fled;
The flame that lit the battle's wreck,
Shone round him o'er the dead.

Yet beautiful and bright he stood,
As born to rule the storm;
A creature of heroic blood,
A proud, though childlike form.

The flames rolled on – he would not go,
Without his father's word;
That father, faint in death below,
His voice no longer heard.

He called aloud – 'Say, father, say
If yet my task is done?'
He knew not that the chieftain lay
Unconscious of his son.

'Speak, father!' once again he cried,
'If I may yet be gone!'
– And but the booming shots replied,
And fast the flames rolled on.

Upon his brow he felt their breath
And in his waving hair;
And look'd from that lone post of death,
In still yet brave despair.

And shouted but once more aloud,
'My father! must I stay?'
While o'er him fast, through sail and shroud,
The wreathing fires made way.

They wrapped the ship in splendour wild,
They caught the flag on high,
And streamed above the gallant child,
Like banners in the sky.

There came a burst of thunder sound –
The boy – oh! where was he?
Ask of the winds that far around
With fragments strewed the sea!

With mast, and helm, and pennon fair,
That well had borne their part,
But the noblest thing which perished there,
Was that young faithful heart.

Ship	Launched	Length	Mainmast Height	Beam	Draught	Max Speed	W/D	Crew	Guns
Mary Rose	1511	105ft (32m) keel*	unknown	39 ft (12m)	15 ft (4.6m)	Unknown	D 500*	415 inc soldiers	36*
The Golden Hind	1577	102 ft (31m)	92 feet (28m)*	20 ft (6.1m)	9 ft (2.7m)*	8 knots*	D 150*	80-85	22
Vasa	1627	226ft (69m)	172ft (52.5m)	38ft (11.7m)	16ft (4.8m)	unknown	D 1,210	145 & 300 soldiers	64
Queen Anne's Revenge	1710	103ft (31.4m)	unknown	24.6ft (7.5m)	unknown	unknown	W 200	300*	30*
HMS Endeavour	1764	97ft 8in (29.77m)	92ft (28m)	29ft 2in (8.89m)	11ft 4in (3.45m)	8 knots	W 366	94	22
HMS Victory	1765	227ft 6 in (69.34m)	205ft (62.5m)	51ft 10in (15.8m)	28ft 9in (8.76m)	11 knots	D 3500	850	100
Santissima Trindida	1769	201ft (61.3m)	250ft (76.2m)*	53ft (16.2m)	26.3ft (8.02m)	9.6 knots	D 4,950	1050	112
USS Constitution	1797	207ft (63m)	220ft (67m)	43ft 6in (13.26m)	23ft (7m)	13 knots	D 2,200	450	52
HMS Pickle	1799	73ft (22.3m)	82ft (25m)	20ft 7in (6.3m)	9ft 6in (2.9m)	14 knots	W 127	40*	6
HMS Beagle	1820	90.3ft (27.5m)	112ft (34.1m)*	24.5ft (7.5m)	12.5ft (3.8m)		W 235	120	10
HMS Warrior	1860	420 ft (128m)	175ft (53.3m)	58ft 4in (17.8m)	26ft 10in (8.2m)	14.5 knots	D 9,137	705	40
Cutty Sark	1869	280ft (85.34m)	152ft (47m)	36ft (10.97m)	20ft (6.1m)	17.5 knots	D 2,100	28-35	0
HMS Dreadnought	1906	527ft (160.6m)		82ft 1in (25.0m)	29ft 7.5in (9m)	21 knots	D 18,410	700-810	37
Titanic	1911	882ft 9in (269.1m)		92ft 6in (28.2m)	34ft 7in (10.5m)	24 knots	D 46,328	892 & 2435 crew	0
HMS Hood	1918	860ft 7in (262.3m)		104ft 2in (31.8m)	32ft (9.8m)	32 knots	D 47,430	1,433	26
Bismarck	1939	823ft 6in (251m)		118ft 1in (36m)	30ft 6in (9.3m)	30 knots	D 41,700	2,065	52
USS Missouri	1944	887ft 3in (270.4m)		108ft 2in (32.97m)	37ft 9in (11.51m)	32.7 knots	D 58,400	2,700	29
Santa María	1492*	161ft (49m) *	82ft (25m)*	18ft (5.5m)*	10ft (3.2m)*	unknown	D 150*	40	4

Ship Comparisons

'*' Indicates an estimated dimension

For length, we have given the total length from forwardmost point of the bowsprit to the taffrail (where applicable)

For weight and displacements, we have given maximum loading figures where possible

For WWII and later, flak guns and torpedo tubes have been excluded from the 'guns' count.

Lengths and Distances

Imperial, Metric, Admiralty Standard. All these, and some more obscure ones, end up with some slightly differing lengths between countries for something with the same name. Here we give what we hope will help your reading for the Age of Sail period.

Fathom

A fathom: a unit to show how deep the water is. A fathom is 6 feet (1.83 metres), and is believed to come from the distance between a man's outstretched arms. Possibly coming from the Anglo-Saxon word for embrace, *faethm*. In Cornwall the fathom was also used to measure the depth of coal seams.

Shackle

Prior to 1949, a shackle was twelve and a half fathoms. The bower cable (the bow anchor cable) came in twelve lengths, with the lengths joined by shackles. These twelve lengths were each twelve and a half fathoms long (75 feet, 22.86 metres), thus defining the length of a single shackle.

After 1949, a shackle was re-defined as 15 fathoms (90 feet, 27.43 metres).

Cable

A cable length (from the length of the main anchor cable) is 608 feet, (185.32 metres), which is one tenth of a nautical mile.

A Nautical Mile

A nautical mile is 1.1508 miles (6080 feet, 1.85 kilometres), and is different to a *'land'* mile as it is used for charts, which allow for the curvature of the earth, and is the distance of one minute of latitude (with some adjustments for the poles). The UK's nautical mile used to be just over a metre longer than the international nautical mile (1853.18 metres as opposed to 1852 metres).

A Knot

A knot is a measurement of speed and is one nautical mile per hour (1.15 mph, 1.85 kph). This comes from when knots were tied into a line (the log line) which was thrown overboard, with the numbers of knots passing through a sailors' hand in a given amount of time showing how fast the ship was travelling.

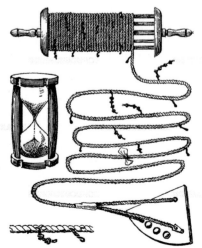

The rope was knotted every 47 feet and 3 inches, and the amount of rope played out was timed to 30 seconds. The complete set-up (see right) is also known as a chip log.

Printed in Poland
by Amazon Fulfillment
Poland Sp. z o.o., Wrocław